D1283903

A
FIRST
EDITION?

A FIRST EDITION?

Statements of selected North American, British Commonwealth, and Irish publishers on their methods of designating first editions

Edited by
Edward N. Zempel
& Linda A. Verkler

The Spoon River Press

Introduction

This reference book is the outgrowth of our collecting interest--modern first editions. A year ago, finding no comprehensive and current guide for identifying American and English first editions, we undertook the project that has become this book.

The project expanded, and we contacted publishers not only in the United States and England, but also in Canada, the Republic of Ireland, Scotland, Australia and New Zealand. We asked each publisher how they designated their first editions.

The term "first edition" is ambiguous. However, to most book collectors, it means "the first printing of the first edition." Thus, in this reference, we have interested ourselves in those methods by which publishers designate the first printing of a first edition. In an attempt to determine this information, there were, in many instances, subsequent inquiries.

Over 550 publishers are listed. We received responses from over 400 American publishers and over 100 English publishers. Most of the statements have been printed exactly as they were received. A few statements--or sections of statements--have been paraphrased. These have no quotation marks. Statements are arranged alphabetically, by publisher, and all foreign countries are indicated. There is an ADDENDA SECTION.

We wish to express our appreciation to the many publishers who responded to our query--or queries.

Edward Zempel
Linda Verkler

June, 1977

A

ABELARD-SCHUMAN LIMITED (ENGLAND)

"We do not identify first editions in any special way but indicate a reprint on the copyright page."

HARRY N. ABRAMS, INC.

"I'm afraid we have had no special policies about citing editions. When we've done it, it's been mostly on textbooks. We are now tending more toward putting First Edition on the copyright page. Again, mostly on textbooks (Janson's History of Art, for one) we give printings and their dates."

ACADEMIC PRESS INC. (LONDON), LTD. (ENGLAND)

"We do not have any special method of identifying first editions of our titles."

ACADEMY EDITIONS (ENGLAND)

"Our first editions carry the following statement on the title verso:
    First published in Great Britain in 19.. by
    Academy Editions
Following reprints have in addition:
    Reprinted in 19..
New editions are similarly indicated with:
    Second edition 19.."

ACROPOLIS BOOKS LTD.

"We only indicate those printings or editions after the first."

ACTIMIC PRESS LTD. (ENGLAND)

See J. Garnet Miller Ltd.

ADDISON HOUSE, PUBLISHERS

"I am afraid that our first edition is probably the same thing as a first printing as most of our books will not warrant change over the years."

ADDISON-WESLEY PUBLISHING COMPANY

"Our present method of identification on printings is
merely an alphabetical and numerical code. This
applies to both our children's books and to our adult
trade books. For instance, on the copyright page of
a new book the code would be listed:
          A B C D E F G H I J K   7 9 8 7
(this indicates a first printing in the year 1977)
    "As each reprint is done, one letter of the alphabet
is dropped and the last number if in a different year.
For instance, a second printing would have
          B C D E F G H I J K   7 9 8
(a second printing in 1978)
    "We do not indicate 'first edition,' 'second edition.'
Some of our earlier children's books have 'first printing,'
'second printing,' etc. Some have no designation
whatsoever."

ADLARD-COLES LTD. (ENGLAND)

See Granada Publishing Limited

AFRICANA PUBLISHING COMPANY

See Holmes and Meier Publishers, Inc.

ALASKA NORTHWEST PUBLISHING COMPANY

"I'm not sure how regular we've been until the last
couple of years, but our current method of designating
1st editions is not to designate them. A second

printing will be marked:
>First printing, date
>Second printing, date

And so on until we do a revised edition. Then it's
>Revised edition, date
>Second printing, revised edition, date."

GEORGE ALLEN & UNWIN LTD. (ENGLAND)

"We identify all our books on the back of the title page by a bibliographical note which declares the date of first publication. Subsequent impressions or editions are noted as and when they occur. A first edition, by which is normally meant a first impression of a first edition will have only a single line entry of first publication with the appropriate date."

J.A. ALLEN & CO., LTD. (ENGLAND)

"Please be advised it is our custom to indicate the date of original publication on the verso of the title page. Where there is a new edition or reprint, it will be indicated below the original copyright notice."

W.H. ALLEN & CO., LTD. (ENGLAND)

"This Company does not have any special method of identifying first editions. So far as I can ascertain, the Company, which dates back to the eighteenth century, has never used any identifying designation."

ALOES BOOKS (ENGLAND)

"We don't have a hard or fast rule on editions. We hardly ever mention state of printing, merely if it's our second print & so on."

AMPHOTO

"No special way of indicating first editions, but second & subsequent editions are so noted. Therefore, absence of any indication (or of multiple copyright dates) usually indicates a first edition. It may also indicate a reprint (unrevised) of the 1st, but this, too, is usually noted."

ANANSI (CANADA)

See House of Anansi Press Limited

ANTHROPOSOPHIC PRESS, INC.

"Because of the particular nature of our publications, we do not identify editions. Even reprintings, when they have continued for decades, are not noted."

ANTONSON PUBLISHING LTD. (CANADA)

"Our only means of designating a first edition is the listing of 'First Printing' and the date of this first printing. We date each additional printing. Usually, this relates to the year shown for the current copyright. Our dating as indicated above is consistent."

APERTURE, INC.

"First printings are usually identified with either 'First Edition' or 'first printing.' Sometimes, as in the case of <u>Ghana</u>, the c/r is used for more than one edition. (There is an English edition as well.) We'll omit the printing; but even here, no absolute rule.

"The phrase 'first published in_____' usually means that this is <u>not</u> the point of first publication-- as, 'first published in Great Britain by Smithy' implies that Smithy is not the first publisher of the book, but the book <u>may</u> be simultaneously published in the U.S. and the book was a U.S. creation.

"When reprint numbers are used, the idea is to simply delete the lowest number from the plate (we don't have to make a new plate) for a reprint. When this method is used, the lowest printing number that can be read is the right one."

THE AQUILA PUBLISHING COMPANY LIMITED (SCOTLAND)

"Our normal practice is to publish books in at least two editions at the same time, occasionally three. These are pamphlet and signed pamphlets (limited edn.) and paperback, hardback (And in most cases signed ltd. hardback). Where a signed edition is published this is taken by the British National Bibliography and the British Library (formerly the publications division of the British Museum) as the first edition, but legally all three (or two) editions are 'first edition'. When we reprint this is <u>always</u> stated in the book, either on the back cover or on the verso title page. Where a second edition is concerned this is also shown. The legal definition of an edition as opposed to a reprint/impression is that an edition must

be re-set either in its whole, or in important parts.
The corrections of errors, or small author's revisions
are normally not enough to make this a new edition, so
long as these are of a very minor nature. First editions
(not anthologies) are always marked as such on the
verso title, and Anthologies have this information
usually in the form of a codicil to the copyright notice."

ARGUS COMMUNICATIONS

"Our first printing is coded on the copyright page in
the following way: 0 1 2 3 4 5 6 7 8 9. Each time we
go back to press one numeral is deleted starting on
the left-hand side."

ARKHAM HOUSE PUBLISHERS, INC.

"All Arkham House books are limited (first) editions
with the exception of the collected works of H.P.
Lovecraft, the subsequent reprintings of which are
acknowledged in the end colophon to each volume."

ART ALLIANCE PRESS

See Associated University Presses, Inc.

ARTISTS AND ALCHEMISTS PUBLICATIONS

"The books printed today, that do not say 'first
printing' -- are a first printing -- in the future we will
indicate such."

ASSOCIATED UNIVERSITY PRESSES, INC.

" In addition to this press (Fairleigh Dickinson University Press) we also administer the affairs of Bucknell University Press, The University of Delaware Press, and the Art Alliance Press. The Presses have no particular means of designating first editions or first printings. However, subsequent editions and printings do carry printing histories."

ATHENEUM PUBLISHERS

"Atheneum's method of designating a first edition is by clearly indicating such on the copyright page.
"It will invariably be found on the last line on the copyright page, and will say 'First Edition' or 'First American Edition' (the latter in the case of a book which has been issued earlier in a foreign country)."

THE ATHLONE PRESS OF THE UNIVERSITY OF LONDON (ENGLAND)

"We add no words to identify first editions of our books. Indeed the absence of description is the identification since all printings subsequent to the first are identified on the verso of the title page. A first edition would therefore bear on the verso of the title page the copyright line © A.N. Other 1976. The second edition would have the words Second Edition on the title page and this information would also be included in the bibliographical details immediately following the copyright line."

THE ATLANTIC MONTHLY PRESS

The edition (e.g. First Edition or First American Edition) is indicated on the copyright page. Subsequent printings of the edition are listed.

AUCKLAND UNIVERSITY PRESS
(NEW ZEALAND)

"First editions are marked e.g. 'First published 1976'; subsequent printings are identified 'Reprinted 1976' or '2nd edition 1976' depending on whether there is new matter or not. We have always used this method."

J.J. AUGUSTIN INCORPORATED PUBLISHER

"<u>All</u> our books are first editions. We never reprint."

B

JOHN BAKER (ENGLAND)

See Adam and Charles Black Publishers

BANYAN BOOKS, INC.

"Our first editions carry the copyright notice alone; subsequent editions are noted (2nd printing, 19-_), (rev. ed. 19__) as the situations warrant."

BARLENMIR HOUSE, PUBLISHERS

"Barlenmir House's method of identifying first editions
in its publications is by identifying 'FIRST EDITION'
on the copyright page of the book."

A.S. BARNES & COMPANY, INC.

"We make no specific identification of first editions
or first printings. Subsequent editions and printings
do carry a printing history on the copyright page."

BARNES & NOBLE BOOKS

"To designate a first edition the words First Edition
are used on the copyright page, although often a first
edition is not designated. The first printing of an
edition is indicated as follows on the copyright page:
    76 77 78 10 9 8 7 6 5 4 3 2 1
The second printing is indicated like this:
    76 77 78 10 9 8 7 6 5 4 3 2
The numbers before 10 indicate years.
Previously printings were listed as follows:
    First printing, July, 1964."

BARRE PUBLISHING CO., INC.

"Every printing after the first is listed with the
edition on the copyright page. (i.e. on the first
edition, first printing, the c/r page says only 1st
edition; on 2nd printing, '2nd printing' is added to
1st edition). This method does not differ from any
previously used."

B.T. BATSFORD, LIMITED (ENGLAND)

First printing of the first edition is designated by
the words: First published 19___.
"The form which this follows is similar to that which
has been Batsford's practice for a good many years
now."

THE BEEHIVE PRESS

"All books are our first editions, unless the copyright page specifically states something like, 'Copyright 1972 by The Beehive Press. Reprinted 1976.'"

BEING PUBLICATIONS

"The act of publication is our method of identifying
a first edition; consecutive editions or printings
are so marked.
"We have not used any different methods."

G. BELL & SONS, LTD. (ENGLAND)

"We do not have any common form of words on the
title page verso of our books relating to the first
edition. We would assume that the copyright line
giving the year would provide the necessary information. Sometimes we add 'First published in (year)',
with or without our name following."

BELLEVUE PRESS

"The colophon page of each of our books clearly

states the information any collector would wish to know about any one of our books. Here we note printer, designer or artist when the particular book requires such notes, and the size of our published editions, noting how many are reserved for 'signed' copies, how many are published in the trade edition, and if the book is other than a first edition."

ERNEST BENN, LTD. (ENGLAND)

"We follow standard practice, e.g. that adopted by University Presses in always stating date of first publication. We always differentiate between a straight reprint, usually referred to as a 'Second impression' etc. and where any revision has taken place 'Second (corrected) impression', and major revision as a 'Second edition.'"

BHAKTIVEDANTA BOOK TRUST

"The printing history of our books is printed on the copyright page of each book. If a book says First Printing, then it is a First Edition. There is no indication as to when a book becomes a Second Edition."

BIG SKY

"I simply say 'First Edition.'"

BINFORD & MORT

"When first publishing under the imprint of Metropolitan Press, our company used the star method to indicate the number of the printing--though when changes in text were made, the book was then stated to be a second edition, etc. One star indicated the first reprinting; two stars, the second, and so on.

"Under Binfords & Mort, we have some books listed under the name of the Metropolitan Press books. Now, under Binford & Mort, the printing or edition is so indicated on the copyright page."

BINFORDS & MORT

See Binford & Mort.

ADAM AND CHARLES BLACK PUBLISHERS LIMITED (ENGLAND)

"We designate a first edition by the words 'First edition (date)' on the biblio page. Subsequently we add the words 'Reprinted (date)' or 'Second edition (date)' etc. These methods of identification do not differ from any previously used, and the same practice is followed by books published by John Baker and Dacre Press."

BLACKBERRY

"All Blackberry books are limited first editions. Any future reprint will, of course, be noted in the book next to the copyright notice."

BLACKIE AND SON LIMITED (SCOTLAND)

"Since the 1957 Copyright Act our imprint or biblio

pages have contained the words, e.g.
© John Hume 1974
First published 1974
and this style may be taken to identify a first edition.
Subsequent editions would have this information plus
the date of the subsequent edition (be it a reprint,
revision or new edition)."

BLACK SPARROW PRESS

"The copyright page of first printings carries no
identifying notation, but first printings always have
a full colophon page, and their title pages are in
color.
"Reprints have the title page in black and white only,
carry no colophon, and are identified as 'Second
printing', 'Third printing', etc., on the copyright
page.
"For further details see Seamus Cooney's <u>A Check-
list of the First One Hundred Publications of the
Black Sparrow Press</u> (Black Sparrow Press, Los Angeles
1971), and its projected successor covering the first
250 titles."

BASIL BLACKWELL & MOTT, LTD. (ENGLAND)

"Before the Universal Copyright Convention of 1957
it was our practice to put the date of publication on
either the recto or verso of the title page, but occasionally for reasons of space it was sometimes transferred
to the back of the book, but only rarely. Since 1957
of course the international copyright mark and the date
of publication appear on the verso of the title page."

BLACKWELL SCIENTIFIC PUBLICATIONS, LTD. (ENGLAND)

"The first editions of our books are identifiable as such only by the absence of any reference to later editions on the title page, recto or verso."

WILLIAM BLACKWOOD & SONS, LTD. (SCOTLAND)

"In the case of a title published by William Blackwood & Sons Ltd., the first edition bears the year of publication below the imprint on the title page. For a reprint the year is removed, and below the copyright note on the verso of the title page, the following note is added: 'Reprinted 19__'. Subsequent reprints are recorded in the same way.

"I should stress that this is our current practice. In the past, especially with the large number of books published by the firm up to about 60 years ago, the system was not consistent. However, I think it is true to say that in the case of a reprint, the above notation, or something similar, was always used. Thus any book which does not bear a reprint note may be assumed to be a first edition. But there were possibly exceptions, and I believe in the early 19th century it was the fashion to attempt to 'establish' a new writer by claiming that his book was already in its second edition whereas in fact it was only the first printing. The first book of John Gibson Lockhart, _Peter's Letters to His Kinsfolk,_ was I think treated in such a way."

BLANDFORD PRESS, LTD. (ENGLAND)

First editions are designated by the words: First

published 19__ .

BLUE WIND PRESS

"Undesignated book = first edition, first printing.
The words 'Second Printing' mean 'of the first edition.'
We sometimes use the following code:
          77 78 79 80 5 4 3 2 1
As is it means first printing, 1977. If we do 2nd
printing in 1977 we erase the '1.' If we do 2nd printing
in 1978 we erase the '1' and the '77.' And so on. As
a rule of thumb I consider a 'new' (2nd, 3rd &c)
edition one in which the text has been altered. A new
cover is simply a new printing to me. But a book re-
typeset for a new format (size) but with the text
unaltered is also a new edition."

THE BODLEY HEAD LIMITED (ENGLAND)

First editions are designated by the words: "First
published 19__ . "

THE BOOKSTORE PRESS

"We have no special methods."

THE BOXWOOD PRESS

"All of our publications are original (not reprints)
and are first editions. Second editions and reprints
are so marked."

THE BRANDEN PRESS, INCORPORATED

"We do not normally designate a first edition of a book unless it is a limited edition. In this case, the details of the limited edition are explained in some detail.

"On the other hand, we frequently indicate on the copyright page the second edition and so forth after the first printing."

BRIGHAM YOUNG UNIVERSITY PRESS

A line similar to the following appears on the copyright page:

          76   2M   12735

On initial printings, the last two digits of the copyright date agree with the number at the left.

BROCKHAMPTON

See Hodder & Stoughton Children's Books

BROOKE HOUSE PUBLISHERS, INC.

"Brooke House books are intended to carry (as an indication of the number of the printing rather than as any indication of edition) a number on the copyright page consisting of an ascending series of ten figures and a descending series of ten figures. The number on the left is the last digit of the year of the printing; the number on the right is the number of the printing. If a printing is made in the same year as the one just before, only the number on the right is deleted in the new printing. E.g., 7890109876 would indicate a 6th

printing in 1977. If a 7th printing were to be made, the
6 would be deleted. -- A second underline would carry
some indication, e.g., Revised Edition, Second Edition,
etc.; again on the copyright page."

THE BROOKINGS INSTITUTION

"We do not explicitly identify first editions, because
with few exceptions we publish only first editions. We
designate printings by a string of numbers on the copyright page, one of which is deleted whenever the book
is reprinted, so that the lowest surviving number indicates the printing in hand. Whenever we do publish
revised, second, or third, etc., editions, we so label
them on the title page, jacket, cover, stamping die,
and foreword; successive printings are indicated as I
describe above. Instead of the row of numbers we used
until seven or eight years ago the device exemplified
by phrases such as 'Second Printing March 1965'; original printings were not so designated."

BROWN, SON & FERGUSON, LTD.
(SCOTLAND)

"In the majority of our publications, on the bibliographical page is always printed either 'First Edition'
or 'First Printed', but in some of our older books which
are non technical, and which have been running for 30
to 40 years, the original printing date has not been
included."

BUCKNELL UNIVERSITY PRESS

See Associated University Presses, Inc.

BURKE PUBLISHING COMPANY, LTD.
(ENGLAND)

"We confirm that our first editions are identified merely by the bye line 'first published....' which appears above the copyright notice in each book we publish.

" The first printing is clearly identified by the fact that no further bibliographical information appears below, whereas on reprints or new editions similar information is printed under this first line, i.e. reprinted plus the date or revised and reprinted plus the date or second edition plus the date, etc."

BURNS & MAC EACHERN LTD. (CANADA)

"We don't designate first editions. We do designate as such all subsequent printings and editions."

C

CAMERON & CO.

"Our method of designating a first edition is simply to print the words 'First Edition' in the book. Subsequent printings are designated as ' Second Edition,' 'Third Edition,' etc."

JONATHAN CAPE LIMITED (ENGLAND)

"Jonathan Cape's books show their bibliographic history on the verso of the title page (i.e. page iv

or 4). The statement begins: 'First published 19__'
and is followed by the copyright line: 'Copyright ©
19__ by---.' The date in both lines is identical. If
the book was first published elsewhere, we then say:
'First published in Great Britain 19__' and the date in
the copyright line will be earlier. For example: 'First
published in Great Britain 1976' 'Copyright © 1973
by---.' Dates of subsequent reprints, new editions
etc., are listed on the same page."

CAPRA PRESS

"We do not designate first editions or first printings,
but we do designate successive editions or printings."

CARATZAS BROTHERS, PUBLISHERS

"We generally do not have any indication for the
first printing of the first edition; subsequent printings
of the first edition, or subsequent editions are so
indicated on the copyright page and/or the title page
(in the case of a second or otherwise revised edition).
As we have been in business only for two years there
are no past inconsistencies , or few other sins to
contend with."

WILLIAM CAREY LIBRARY

"We have no particular way of designating first
editions of our books. The copyright page will simply
have the copyright notice and date, and the ISBN and
Library of Congress Catalog number. However, subsequent printings and editions are designated as 'Second
printing 1976', etc."

CAROLRHODA BOOKS, INC.

In the past, first printings have been designated by the copyright date alone.

"In subsequent printings, the following was added to the copyright entry:

Second Printing 1977
Third Printing 1979
(and so forth)

"We recently have begun adding a number code to the first printings of each book following the copyright entry:

76 77 78 79 80 10 9 8 7 6 5 4 3 2 1

"When a book is reprinted for the second time, for instance, we remove the '1' and the year of the first printing."

ROBT. CARRUTHERS & SONS (SCOTLAND)

"We have no special way of identifying any 'first editions' of the few works we publish. In fact, except for 'The Scottish War of Independence' by Evan M. Barron, they are all 'first editions,' and in its case the second edition is identifiable by its long special introduction, which really makes it more valuable historically and authoritatively than the first! It is also out of print. So in all other cases whatever date may appear with the imprint, or elsewhere, is the date of first publication."

CASSELL AND COMPANY LTD. (ENGLAND)

"The only means of identification of first editions of our publications is the statement on page iv (the history page) : First published 1976

"The only departure from this is when the book is not first published in this country in which case our history page reads:

First published in Great Britain 1976
"This has always been our practice."

THE CATHOLIC UNIVERSITY OF AMERICA PRESS

"Most of the books published by our firm are printed on a one-time basis. However, a few have been reprinted or revised. In the case of reprinting, we merely state on the copyright page: 'reprinted (date).' With a revised edition, we place on the title page either the words 'newly revised edition' or 'revised and enlarged edition', whichever the case may be."

THE CAXTON PRINTERS, LTD.

"All of our first editions are identified by the absence of any information regarding printings on the copyright page.
"In the case of a second printing or second edition etc., you will find on the copyright page a listing of printings or editions such as this:

First Printing July, 1945
Second Printing August, 1947 etc."

CELESTIAL ARTS

Previously, all printings were listed. As of January 1966, the printing, month, and year are given. A numerical system of one through seven and a series of corresponding dates are given as well:

First Printing, May 1976

1 2 3 4 5 6 7 - 81 80 79 77 76

The first number and the last date designate the printing and date of the current publication.

CENTAUR PRESS, LTD. (ENGLAND)

"Only by omission, as it were. That is to say, a first edition would carry the line (e.g.) © Centaur Press Ltd. 1976.

"A second or subsequent edition would have a line to say so: E.g., 'Second edition 1978.'"

CENTER FOR CONTEMPORARY POETRY

"We only do one edition of 500 copies of each _Voyages_."

CENTER FOR SOUTHERN FOLKLORE

"No designation of first printings and/or editions is used. Will be indicated only on printings and/or editions after the first. This hasn't been implemented yet as we are new in publishing and problem hasn't yet arisen."

W. & R. CHAMBERS, LTD. (SCOTLAND)

"In all our current publications the first date of publication is usually printed on the reverse of the title page along with the copyright notice. Prior to the institution of the copyright notice we normally put in the date of the latest edition or reprint. However in our early publications very often no date was given and therefore first dates of publication are very difficult to identify."

CHATTO AND WINDUS LTD. (ENGLAND)

"We have no particular method beyond ensuring that every book carries the date of first publication, and reprints, whether new impressions or new editions, are clearly listed on the verso of the title page."

CHILDRENS PRESS

"Childrens Press uses the dateline designation. For example:
     1 2 3 4 5 6 7 8 9 10 11 12 R 78 77 76 75
"The digits to the left of the letter R (reprint) indicate the printing. The digits to the right of the letter R indicate the year. The above was first printed in 1975. In the following example, in 1975 the title was printed for the 7th time.
7 8 9 10 11 12 13 14 15 16 17 18 19 20 21 22 23 24 25 R 75
"Elk Grove and Golden Gate Junior Books published since we acquired those companies also carry this dateline designation. Titles published prior to our acquisition do not carry any printing designation."

CHILTON BOOK COMPANY

"Chilton Book Company indicates year of publication and number of printing by a numerical code. First number indicates publication year, last indicates

printing. e.g.
```
        7 8 9 0 1 2 3 4 5 6       0 9 8 7 6 5 4 3 2 1
        published in 1977          first printing
```
"Second and additional revised editions are usually noted on both title page and copyright page."

THE CHRISTOPHER PUBLISHING HOUSE

"No set policy, usually second editions and second printings are indicated on copyright page."

CHRISTOPHER'S BOOKS

"Christopher's Books does not indicate 1st edition or printing; we have never done a 2nd, but would indicate a 2nd printing or edition if we were to produce one."

CHRONICLE BOOKS

"Our first editions can be identified by the lack of any edition imprint. Subsequent editions are indicated on the copyright page.

"We specify all subsequent 'printings' after the first one. When it is a new 'edition', we so specify. So, first printings of the first editions are the only books that do not carry a printing or edition reference."

CHURCHILL LIVINGSTONE

See Longman, Inc.

CITADEL PRESS

"It is our normal practice to print the words First Edition on the copyright page."

CITY LIGHTS BOOKS, INC.

"We don't really have a method. Most of our books state Second printing, third printing, etc., but sometimes a new printing has been done without a notice. Usually the absence of any identifying statement would indicate a first printing of a first edition."

ARTHUR H. CLARK COMPANY

"We designate first editions by using only one date on the copyright page. If the edition is a 2nd, it is so stated on the copyright page."

T. & T. CLARK LIMITED (SCOTLAND)

"All our first editions will have simply the date of publication or 'first printed---'. All subsequent editions will have the date of first, latest and intervening editions clearly set out."

CLAY PUBLISHING CO., LTD. (CANADA)

All printings after the first are designated by month and year.

CLEARWATER PUBLISHING CO., INC.

"We do not mark our first editions First Edition;
Subsequent editions are marked second edition and so
on. If there are no changes in the book, the second
printing is considered part of the first edition and is
marked, Second Printing."

THE COACH HOUSE PRESS (CANADA)

"Some books the first edition was numbered by
machine. None have said 'First Edition'. Some books
had letterpress first editions and offset second or
silkscreen and offset. 'Second Printing' and date are
usually put in the colophon."

COBBLESMITH

"We have no special marks."

REX COLLINGS, LTD. (ENGLAND)

"The only information we print in the first edition of
any of our publications is the year in which the book
is published. This follows the name of the copyright
holder (Rex Collings or the author) and appears on the
title verso, as:
© Rex Collings 1976
"All subsequent editions or reprints carry the impression or edition number in addition to the year of original
publication."

THE COLONIAL WILLIAMSBURG FOUNDATION

Currently, first printings are not designated. Subsequent printings are so designated; as well as new or revised editions. In the past, second printings, revised editions, etc., were not always designated.

COLORADO ASSOCIATED UNIVERSITY PRESS

"We have no particular method of identifying first editions. . . . we are a small operation and seldom reprint."

COLUMBIA UNIVERSITY PRESS

"We make a careful distinction between the terms 'printing' and 'edition' -- a 'second printing' is merely a happy reprinting (with errata corrected) of a book that has sold rather well and is indicated by the disappearance of the '1' from the string of numbers on the copyright page; a 'second edition' means that the text has been extensively overhauled, perhaps even chapters added. The latter is indicated by the words 'Second Edition' on the title page and the dates of the first and second editions on the copyright page."

COMMONWEALTH PRESS

"At CP first editions carry no designation. Second, third, fourth, etc., editions are so designated. We have always used this system."

LEO COOPER LTD. (ENGLAND)

See Seeley, Service & Cooper Ltd.

COPPER CANYON PRESS

"Since all our titles to date have been first editions,
we make no notice of same. When (this winter) we
DO make a second printing, it will be so stated on the
copyright page. We also do very limited editions
signed and handbound on most titles. These, of course,
are distinguished by the poet's signature and by the
binding itself."

CORNELL MARITIME PRESS, INC.

"We do not use any specific method other than indicating later printings as <u>Second Printing,</u> etc."

CORNELL UNIVERSITY PRESS

"A book published by Cornell University is a first
edition unless stated otherwise. It is also a first
printing unless stated otherwise."

THE COUNTRYMAN PRESS, INC.

"The Countryman Press does nothing to indicate a
first edition in the original printing. On a subsequent
printing, there is noted 'second printing' with the
date, or 'revised edition'. Anything other would be
considered a first edition."

COURIER OF MAINE BOOKS

"Our first editions and their first printings are designated in no special way. They simply carry on the
copyright page a standard copyright notice, the ISBN,
and LC number. These methods do not differ from any
previously used."

CRAFTSMAN BOOK COMPANY

"We make no effort to identify first editions."

CRITERION BOOKS

See Thomas Y. Crowell Company

CROSBY LOCKWOOD STAPLES (ENGLAND)

See Granada Publishing Limited

THE CROSSING PRESS

"The only way we designate 1st editions is the
omission of 2nd printing, 3rd printing, so on. (or 2nd
edition, 3rd edition). Am I clear? When we rerun
a book, we place the date of the rerunning & the words
2nd or 3rd printing or edition."

THOMAS Y. CROWELL COMPANY

"On first editions, the numbers 1 2 3 4 5 6 7 8 9 10

appear at the bottom of the page. Each time the book
is reprinted, the next number is deleted, thus designating the current printing. A long time ago, I believe
the previous method was to say: 'First printing',
'Second printing', etc."

D

DACRE PRESS (ENGLAND)

See Adam and Charles Black, Publishers

THE DARTNELL CORPORATION

"First printing of a first edition designated by copyright date only. This has always been our standard
practice."

DAUGHTERS OF ST. PAUL

"Our first editions may be designated by the copyright date on the page after the title page."

DAVID & CHARLES (HOLDINGS) LTD.
(ENGLAND)

"We only identify first editions by providing the
usual ' © John Smith 1976' on the back of the title
page; any subsequent impressions or editions would
be identified as such, with their date. So the absence
of any note such as 'second impression' conveys that

the book is in fact a first impression."

PETER DAVIES LTD. (ENGLAND)

"We have no means of identifying first editions
other than the obvious bibliographical information
provided on the verso title page of all our books."

DAVIS-POYNTER LIMITED (ENGLAND)

"We have no particular method of identifying first
editions. We use the normal international copyright
line, that is the details of copyright holder and date.
Any reprints have another date line."

THE DAWN HORSE PRESS

"We originally published in hard cover, The Knee of
Listening, by Franklin Jones. To identify our first
edition, this first publication was printed by CSA Press,
Lakemont, GA 30552. This is the distinguishing
characteristic of the first edition of the publication.
All our other publications are duly marked, 1st edition,
2nd edition, etc."

DAWSON'S BOOK SHOP

"We do not identify first editions of our publications
since we very seldom reprint our titles. In the few
instances when they have been reissued, the later
edition is clearly indicated."

THE JOHN DAY CO., INC.

See Thomas Y. Crowell Company

DEAN & SON LTD. (ENGLAND)

"As we are in the mass children's book market we do not publish special first editions.
"Generally speaking, we do an initial large run and do not reprint except in special circumstances."

DECEMBER PRESS

"We designate only those printings and/or editions after the first, and so far we haven't had any of those."

JOHN DE GRAFF, INC.

"We do not have an unvarying procedure to identify which of our books are first editions and which ones are reprints.
"Normally a reprint is indicated on the copyright page by 'reprinted and year' but there are occasions like book club printings and oversights when the copyright page is not changed."

DELACORTE PRESS

See Seymour Lawrence Incorporated

T.S. DENISON & CO., INC.

"We do very little in this regard. We do designate

second, third, fourth etc. printings on the copyright
page, but usually do nothing to designate a first
edition other than the standard book # and copyright
date. In the publishing of special edition books
we assign registration numbers. This is usually a
limited printing."

DENLINGER'S PUBLISHERS

"We do not include a statement in our books to
identify first editions. We identify second editions
or other later editions through inclusion of additional
dates in the copyright statement. A single copyright
date in one of our books indicates that the book is a
first edition.
"Second printings or other later printings are identified through inclusion of the words 'Second Printing'
or other later printing on the copyright page."

J.M. DENT & SONS LTD. (ENGLAND)

"We do not have any set formula for identifying our
first editions, but these normally carry (on the title
verso) the statement 'First published 19__'.
"Where a previously published title is to appear for
the first time in a new format or series, we usually
make the statement 'First published in this edition
19__.'"

DESERET BOOK COMPANY

"We do not make a designation for first edition;
however, if the date of publication on the title page
is the same as the copyright date, it is a first edition.

If the book is reprinted, the date of publication on the
title page will be changed to correspond to the reprint
date. We do not indicate a revised edition unless
substantial copy changes are made."

ANDRE DEUTSCH LTD. (ENGLAND)

"Our normal practice is to print our copyright notice
on the imprint page (i.e. the reverse of the title page).
This will normally read:

> First published 19___by
> Andre Deutsch Limited
> (etc.)

"If we do a reprint then a further line would be added
saying

> Second impression 19___.

"In other words, the first edition is not identified as
such but merely by the absence of any reference to
further printings, revised editions etc."

THE DEVIN-ADAIR COMPANY, INC.

"In almost all instances the second and subsequent
printings carry the notation second printing on the
copyright page."

THE DIAL PRESS

"We designate a first printing of a first edition by
writing 'First printing 19___' on the copyright page."

DODD, MEAD & COMPANY, INC.

"We generally do not mark a book's first edition
nor do we usually mark second and later printings,
although there are exceptions to this practice and there
seems to be no consistency about doing so. Naturally,
if a second printing is marked, the absence of such
notice would indicate a first edition. Any notice of
editions would appear as such on the copyright page.

"We would only be certain to mark a second edition
if there were changes extensive enough to warrant a
change in the copyright notice and the second edition
came out in a year different from the first."
See ADDENDA SECTION.

THE DOLMEN PRESS LIMITED
(REPUBLIC OF IRELAND)

"We are publishing this autumn (1976) a bibliography
of our Press in which all our first editions are identified."

THE DOLPHIN BOOK CO., LTD.
(ENGLAND)

"We have no particular identifying method for defining
first editions. Only when a second edition is published
we state on the verso of the title page the date of the
first edition. Otherwise it is understood that the book
is a first edition, and we always mention the date of
publication."

DORSEY PRESS

" First editions have only Title & author's name
on the cover. Second & subsequent editions are
identified by placing appropriate designation after
the title on the cover & title page.
"First printings & their dates we identify as such by
a statement (example: First Printing, January 1976)
which appears under the copyright declaration."

DOUBLEDAY & COMPANY INC.

"We designate First Editions on the copyright page
thus: FIRST EDITION. On subsequent printings this
is removed."

DOUGLAS-WEST PUBLISHERS, INC.

"The first copies of a new title are normally designated 'First Printing' or 'First Edition' if we anticipate
the title going into several printings. If the book
carries an expensive list price and is likely to become
a collector's item, we designate the first printing as
'First Edition.' Most publishers, we find, use the
two terms interchangeably; in other words, First Printing or First Edition means the same thing."

DOVER PUBLICATIONS, INC.

"We do not distinguish in any way between the first
and subsequent printings of our publications."

DREENAN PRESS, LTD.

"All of our book printings, whether 1st editions or subsequent ones bear the 10 9 8 7 6 5 4 3 2 1 indicators on the copyright page. The last numeral that appears is the number of the printing. E.G. if the copyright page reads 10 9 8 7 6 then the copy is from the sixth printing of that edition.
"Only revised editions (not reprints) bear the info. as to edition and that is on the title page. If no info. appears on title page then it is a first edition."

JAMES DUFFY & CO., LTD.
(REPUBLIC OF IRELAND)

"Our only method is to print the year on the cover and inside title. For reprints we put:
First published 1976
Reprinted 1977
Reprinted 1978
"On the reprints we would omit the year on the cover and inside title."

DUKE UNIVERSITY PRESS

"Although we customarily note a second or later edition or second or later printing as such, we have no particular means of noting a first edition."

DUQUESNE UNIVERSITY PRESS

"There has been no consistent method used to identify first editions of Duquesne University Press titles. For the most part, however, first editions can be

identified by the notation 'first printing' which, when
used, appears on the copyright page. In instances
where there is no indication of the edition or number
of printings, there is no doubt that the book is a first
edition.

"If a book has been revised and a new edition printed,
the information is always registered on the title page.
The number of printings of the new edition is notated on
the copyright page."

E

THE EAKINS PRESS

"In fact Eakins publications are not intended to go
into editions beyond the first, and consequently no
particular mark of identification is accorded the first
printing."

THE ECCO PRESS

"Starting with our spring, 1977 books, all copyright
pages will run the line 'FIRST EDITION' when it is
applicable. Previously, we have not run this line.
However, if any of our books should go into a second
printing, we will run the line 'SECOND EDITION.'"

WM. B. EERDMANS PUBLISHING COMPANY

"We never explicitly state the appearance of a first
edition. The absence of any identifying statement
would indicate the first printing of a first edition.

All other printings of a first edition are indicated as such. Revised editions are explicitly identified."

PAUL ELEK LIMITED (ENGLAND)

"We have no method of identifying first editions."

ELK GROVE BOOKS

See Childrens Press

EMERSON BOOKS, INC.

"We make no specific identification mark on our first editions and to the best of my knowledge have never done so.
"We do identify subsequent editions marking each by the number of its printing. For example--
2nd Printing 1943
3rd Printing 1967
"In some instances we eliminate reference to previous printings but always identify with the current printing."

PAUL S. ERIKSSON, INC.

"We customarily make no mention of first editions or first printings. We do make an attempt to print notices on the © page designating which printing of a particualr edition it is--after the first printing. On editions, we mention revisions only; e.g. © 1971. Revised Edition, 1976."

M. EVANS AND COMPANY, INC.

"We do not designate first editions as separate from
first printings. Our printing history is usually listed
on the very last line of the copyright page. For example:
'9 8 7 6 5 4 3 2 1' means that it is the first printing.
No other use of words such as 'First Edition' is used.
If the right hand digit is deleted, the final digit is the
printing. For example, if the final digit is 2, it is the
second printing."

EVANS BROTHERS LIMITED (ENGLAND)

"The method we follow in Evans is to include the
year of first publication i.e.
>   First published 1976 by
>   Evans Brothers Limited,
>   Montague House,
>   Russell Square,
>   London WCIB 5BX.
"For a reprint we would add the words 'reprint' and
the date for the reprint under the above."

HUGH EVELYN LTD. (ENGLAND)

"The imprint carries the words 'first published in
19__'. Any subsequent printing or new edition would
carry the same statement followed by the year of the
new printing."

EYRE METHUEN LTD. (ENGLAND)

"Beyond the usual information about publisher and
publication date, and the date of the copyright, we
do not have any particular method of identifying

first editions."

F

FABER AND FABER LTD., PUBLISHERS (ENGLAND)

"Our practice here is to print on the back of the title page 'First Published in 19...by Faber and Faber Ltd.' That seems quite straightforward and is in fact so for all books originating here. But there is a slight difficulty that has to be watched. We sometimes use exactly the same formula for books that have already been published in the United States by an American publisher. This may seem a little odd at first, but you will see that it is quite justifiable if you rearrange the words: that is to say, 'First Published by Faber and Faber Ltd. in 19...' Sometimes we do add 'First Published in the United States of America' which makes the situation clear.

"I have two new books in front of me at the moment which illustrate the situation. The first is EZRA POUND: THE LAST ROWER by C. David Heymann where you will find on the verso of the title page the following:
'First Published in Great Britain in 1976 by
Faber and Faber Ltd.'
and lower down
'First Published in United States of America 1976'
"I am not sure whether this does everything that is necessary, but at least it indicates that there is an American publication the date of which has to be checked. The second book is NUREYEV: ASPECTS OF THE DANCER by John Percival where we don't say that the book was first published in the United States,

though in fact the first edition was published by
Putnam's in 1975. There is a special reason for this
because the book originated with us and we sold the
rights to Putnam's, who published it very quickly.
We published later and included some additional
material, so the copyright notice reads: © 1975 and
1976 by John Percival.

"All I want to do in drawing attention to these points
is to warn you that in cases where there is an American
edition it is as well to check carefully when it was
published.

"I might mention that for books by T.S. Eliot published
after he became a director of this firm and published
all his books through us, we always arranged that the
English edition should be published at least a day
before the American edition and thus the English edition
becomes the real first edition.

"But as I said at the beginning of this letter, the
collector must really be prepared to do a bit of work
in order to make sure what he is getting hold of.

"In some ways the real question to be considered is,
how are subsequent editions described? We always
take care to indicate second, third impression or
whatever it may be, or second, third, fourth edition
if there has been an alteration in the text. I think you
will find that this rule is carefully followed.

"In the case of translations, we give the title of the
original and if possible the place of publication and
the name of the publisher."

FABIAN SOCIETY (ENGLAND)

"We have no special method of identifying first
editions. However, they can easily be identified
as subsequent editions would contain the information
that the particular pamphlet or book was reprinted."

FAIRLEIGH DICKINSON UNIVERSITY PRESS

See Associated University Presses, Inc.

FARRAR, STRAUS & GIROUX, INC.

"In answer to your query, we designate first editions by saying just that, plus the year of publication on the copyright pages of our books. An earlier method was to use the words 'first printing.'"

FREDERICK FELL PUBLISHERS, INC.

"We use 1 2 3 4 5 6 7 8 9 0. When reprinted, we delete figure 1, etc., insert 2nd, 3rd, etc., printing on copyright page, change copyright year to Roman numerals."

THE FEMINIST PRESS

"First printing of first edition just says first edition --subsequent printings say first edition, second printing, etc."

FIDES PUBLISHERS, INC.

"We do not identify first editions in any particular way. Revised editions are usually noted on the back cover."

FILTER PRESS

"Generally our first printings are 500 copies, and

are so identified as 'First Printing, date, 1957,' etc.
on the reverse of the title page. As succeeding
printings are made they are not identified in most
cases. The lateness of the printing can usually be
determined by the fact that on the reverse of the title
page we print a list of our WILD & WOOLLY WEST
SERIES in chrono order, and the imprint date of latest
on it shows it was ready at the time of that printing.
For internal use we also use a digit such as 512 or
608, which indicates that particular printing was
done on December of 1975 or August of 1976, etc.
A single digit, such as 1 or 1/2 in lower right part
of reverse of title page shows the size of the press
run in thousands. We're pretty small, so rarely run
more than 1500 or so at a time."

FINE ARTS MUSEUMS OF SAN FRANCISCO

"We use no designation to indicate a first edition
or a first printing. We note subsequent editions and
printings as they occur."

FORDHAM UNIVERSITY PRESS

"The first editions of books published by Fordham
University Press carry the year of publication at the
bottom of the imprint on the title page. This year will
coincide with the year of (first) copyright. The publication and copyright information on the copyright page
always carries enough information to enable the
bibliographer to determine the edition or printing in
his hands. A first edition is usually described as
such, or no statement of edition is present; both
carry equal weight. Our reprints or revisions are
always designated as such: the year of first publi-

cation is either removed from the imprint on the title page or replaced by the new year of republication; the copyright information always carries a complete, if brief, printing history, specifying the years of editions, reprintings, and revisions."

THE GORDON FRASER GALLERY LTD. (ENGLAND)

"We designate first editions simply by having the words 'first published 19___' on the copyright page. Any subsequent editions or reprints would include further information e.g. 'reprinted 19___' or 'new edition 19___'."

W.H. FREEMAN AND COMPANY, PUBLISHERS

All editions after the first are indicated. Printings are not designated. These methods do not differ from any previously used.

SAMUEL FRENCH, INC.

"There is no way that I can answer you but to say that our reprints are not marked as such and our first printings are not marked as such. There is no difference between either, and we do not indicate a difference."

ELEANOR FRIEDE, INC.

"I am an associate publisher with Delacorte Press,

and we indicate First Printing on all books published
first in America."

FRIENDS OF THE EARTH, INC.

"Briefly, we publish two main lines of picture books,
the Earth's Wild Places series (eight volumes now
published) and the Celebrating the Earth series (three
volumes in six editions now published). Each of the
CTE books (Only a little planet, Song of the Earth
Spirit and Of all things most yielding) have been
published in hard and paperback; there is no way to
tell from colophons or other marks between the various
printings, so far as I know.

"On the Earth's Wild Places Series no attempt has
been made to systematically distinguish between the
editions, but it is possible, by comparing colophons
and spines, and by the fact that second editions do
not have spot-varnished pages. By title, this is what
I'd recommend a first edition seeker seek:

RETURN TO THE ALPS:
Colophon: (or publisher's note, as it is called in all
FOE books) includes the phrase 'Color separations
and lithography by Imprimeries Reunies SA, Lausanne.'
Spine: Friends of the Earth
Second and subsequent editions:
Colophon: says 'Lithographed and bound by Arnoldo
Mondadori Editore, Verona'
Spine: Friends of the Earth, Seabury Press
Copyright page says 'This ... printing contains cor-
rections of minor errors but no substantive changes
in text, photographs, or other illustrations.'
EARTH AND THE GREAT WEATHER:
Colophon: says 'printed by Imprimeries Reunies SA,
Lausanne ... color separations by Gravure De Schutter

NV, Antwerp.'
Spine: Friends of the Earth, McCall
Second edition:
Colophon: says 'lithographed and bound by Arnoldo
Mondadori Editore, Verona.'
Spine: Friends of the Earth, Seabury Press
Copyright page includes same statement as RETURN TO
THE ALPS.
  A SENSE OF PLACE:
Colophon: lithography and bound by Arnoldo Mondadori,
color separations by Gravure De Schutter
Spine: Friends of the Earth, Saturday Review Press
Second and subsequent editions:
Colophon: lithographed and bound by Arnoldo Mondadori
Editore, Verona
Spine: Friends of the Earth, Seabury Press
Copyright page includes the same statement as RETURN
TO THE ALPS.
  MAUI: THE LAST HAWAIIAN PLACE
Colophon: 'It was printed on Champion Kromekote by
Barnes Press, Inc., New York City. It was double-
spread collated and bound in Columbia Mills' Sampson
linen by Sendor Bindery, New York City.'
Spine: Friends of the Earth, McCall
Second and Subsequent editions:
Colophon: 'lithographed and bound by Arnoldo
Mondadori Editore, Verona.'
Spine: Friends of the Earth, Seabury Press
Copyright page includes the same statement as RETURN
TO THE ALPS.
  PRIMAL ALLIANCE: EARTH AND OCEAN
(I don't have a copy at hand to check, but believe the
colophon credits the color separations to H.S. Crocker
Company in Burlingame, California, and the spine
probably says Friends of the Earth, Saturday Review
Press).

<u>Second and subsequent editions</u>:
Colophon: lithographed and bound by Arnoldo
Mondadori Editore, Verona
Spine: Friends of the Earth, Seabury Press
Copyright page: same statement as RETURN TO THE
ALPS; copyright page is the same page with
'Contents.'

   On the following three titles there have been no
second editions:
   ERYRI: THE MOUNTAINS OF LONGING
<u>Colophon</u>: lithographed by Arnoldo Mondadori Editore,
Verona ... color separated by Gravure De Schutter NV,
Antwerp
<u>Spine</u>: FOE, McCall, George Allen & Unwin
   GUALE: THE GOLDEN COAST OF GEORGIA
<u>Colophon</u>: lithographed and bound by Arnoldo
Mondadori Editore, Verona
<u>Spine</u>: Friends of the Earth, Seabury Press
   MICRONESIA: ISLAND WILDERNESS
Colophon and spine are the same as GUALE: THE
GOLDEN COAST OF GEORGIA

I should point out that all books with Seabury Press
on the spine also have 'A Continuum Book' on the
title page.
   "We will be bringing out a limited-edition called
HEADLANDS (signed and numbered, 700 for sale) in
October, 1976."

FUNK & WAGNALLS PUBLISHING COMPANY

   See Thomas Y. Crowell Company

G

GAMBIT, INC.

"We continue to identify first editions as we always have by carrying the words First Printing in a separate line above the copyright notice."

GEOGRAPHICAL PUBLICATIONS LIMITED (ENGLAND)

No particular methods are used.

GEORGIA STATE UNIVERSITY, SCHOOL OF BUSINESS ADMINISTRATION, PUBLISHING SERVICES DIVISION

"Our approach to designating a first edition, first printing is by the absence of a designation. Only the second and succeeding editions and printings carry these notices--verso title page."

GILL AND MACMILLAN LTD. (REPUBLIC OF IRELAND)

"We do not in fact have any particular method of identifying first editions of our books. The relevant information is included on the reverse title, or imprint, page of each book we publish."

GLIDE PUBLICATIONS

"No mention is made of <u>any</u> edition unless there is a Revised Edition, which is so indicated."

GOLDEN GATE JUNIOR BOOKS

See Childrens Press

GOLDEN PRESS

See Western Publishing Company, Inc.

GOLDEN WEST BOOKS

"The first edition is the first printing of a book. It lacks any comment on the copyright page. As it receives a second printing it is noted here that this happens to be the second printing and the date. If it is revised it so states."

VICTOR GOLLANCZ LTD. (ENGLAND)

"The only way to identify a Gollancz first edition is the negative one of seeing that there is no reference to a second or subsequent impression or a revised edition or a reissue on the verso of the title page."

GRANADA PUBLISHING (ENGLAND)

"Our first editions are identified in the copyright notice appearing in the prelims of every book which of

course incorporates the year of publication. Re-issues
and reprints can easily be identified by a statement
to this effect which would appear within the copyright
notice which will also incorporate a statement as to
the date the book was first published.

WARREN H. GREEN, INC.

"First editions are not identified in any way. On the
copyright page we simply put © (date), Warren H.
Green, Inc.
"Then on the Title Page and on the Copyright Page,
each straight reprinting is noted as 'second printing,'
'third printing,' etc.
"If a printing is revised but not sufficiently to call it
a new edition, on the Title Page and Copyright Page
it is identified as 'Revised First Printing,' 'Revised
Second Printing,' whatever applies.
"For new editions, on both the Title Page and the
Copyright Page, we simply put new copyright information, i.e., ' © second edition.'"

THE STEPHEN GREENE PRESS

"At the present time, we run a printing code line at
the foot of the copyright page. Starting at the left,
it shows printing numbers 1 through 9; and then, starting from the right it shows the current year and 5 or 6
succeeding years--as follows:
   1 2 3 4 5 6 7 8 9 80 79 78 77 76
"The first printing carries the entire code line. The
second printing carries the entire line minus the figure
1, and, if necessary, minus as many year figures at
the end to make the line end with the current year.

So that a third printing in 1979 would look like this:
3 4 5 6 7 8 9 80 79

"We do not now have any particular method of identifying first editions (as distinct from initial printings).
We do identify subsequent editions--e.g., 'second
edition,' 'first revised edition,' and the like. But for
the most part our first editions are identified by the
absence of any statement identifying them as anything
but a first edition."

GREENWOOD PRESS, INC.

The first printing of a first edition is designated
by: "First published in 19___." All printings thereafter
are indicated.

Revised editions and editions after the first are
indicated on the copyright page.

GROSSMAN PUBLISHERS

"There is no designation for the first edition of
Grossman Publishers' books. Other printings are so
indicated on the copyright page."

GROVE PRESS, INC.

"All our books carry a printing history on their copyright page.

"The legend says 'First Printing,' 'Second Printing,'
etc. This means of identification has been in use at
Grove at least since 1970."

GRUNE & STRATTON, INC.

"The last page of the index has a code, a lettered code. 'A' is a first printing; 2nd printing, the 'A' is deleted and the top letter is 'B', etc.

"Following editions become part of the title of the book."

H

E.M. HALE & COMPANY

"We do not identify a first edition, but we do identify subsequent printings: 'Second printing,' 'Third printing,' etc. Our books are published under the imprint of Harvey House, Publishers."

ROBERT HALE LIMITED (ENGLAND)

"There is not a great deal I can say about our method of identifying first editions. This is mainly by implication. The first bibliographical line that appears on our imprint page is, for example, 'first published in Great Britain 1976'. If there is no following bibliographical detail the book is our first edition. Publication or prior publication in another country would be noted if the book were a translation. In the case of publication in English (in America, for instance) there would not necessarily be a mention unless it originally appeared under another title.

"It is necessary to read the bibliographical details in conjunction with the copyright line which in the case of prior publication in America will have a different date from the British publication date.

"As a matter of interest a considerable number of books produced by us which appeared both in America and Britain have joint imprints on all copies."

HAMISH HAMILTON LTD. (ENGLAND)

"The only method of identifying first impressions (I think this is safer nomenclature than 'editions') is to say 'first published in Great Britain 19__ by Hamish Hamilton Limited'. Any further impressions are simply along the lines of 'second impression July 1976', etc."

HANGING LOOSE PRESS

"We only started publishing books about a year ago and have yet to reprint a book. When we do, I suppose we will add 'Second Printing'. There is nothing in the original copies of the first 6 titles to indicate that they are first editions or first printings."

HARPER & ROW, PUBLISHERS, INC.

" The copyright page says 'First Edition.'
Under that is a chain of numbers, 76 77 78 79 9 8 7 etc.

"As a book reprints, the First Edition line gets dropped and so do the outdated numbers.

"A book in its third printing in 1976 would have a line that looks like:

76   77   78   79   9 8 7 6 5 4 3 ."

GEORGE G. HARRAP & COMPANY LTD.
(ENGLAND)

"The method which we ... use to identify first
editions, is to print the publication date; any reprint
dates follow this date in subsequent impressions, as
do the dates of new or revised editions."

HART-DAVIS, MACGIBBON LIMITED
(ENGLAND)

See Granada Publishing Limited

HART PUBLISHING CO., INC.

"We do not indicate the printings or editions in any
of our books."

HARVARD BUSINESS SCHOOL
DIVISION OF RESEARCH

"We use no unusual identification for First Editions:
the date of publication on the title page. Second,
Third, etc., Printings are noted on the Copyright Page.
"Date of publication is on title page of all printings.
The absence of a 2nd printing, etc., on copyright
page does not necessarily assure the reader of 1st
ptg. of 1st edition."

HARVARD UNIVERSITY PRESS

"We do not have a special way of identifying first
editions. In other words, if the edition is not identified as second or revised, it is a first edition. The

first printing of the first edition carries the same date on the title page as on the copyright notice. When the edition is reprinted, the printing is identified on the copyright page, as, for example, Second printing, 1976, and the date on the title page is deleted. A second edition is called that on the title page and dated. If a second edition is reprinted, the words 'second printing' refer to a reprint of the second edition."

HASTINGS HOUSE, PUBLISHERS, INC.

"First printings are identified only by the copyright notice. Subsequent printings give date. Subsequent editions so state and give date."

HAWTHORN BOOKS, INC.

"Although Hawthorn does not use the phrase 'First Edition' on its copyright page, we do have a method of identifying various printings of a book. At the foot of the copyright page we set Arabic numerals from one to ten. For the second printing we delete the one, etc., so that the first number indicates the number of the printing.

"According to copyright law, a specified amount of material in a book must be completely new if a book is to be considered a second edition. On any title for which these requirements are fulfilled, we print the words 'Second Edition' on the jacket, title page, and copyright page. This second edition is not, however, indicated in the Arabic numbering codes. The first printing of the second edition would simply list all the numbers from one to ten again, indicating that it was the first printing of the second edition.

A revised or updated edition of a book will be so listed on the jacket, title page, and copyright page-- just as with a second edition. But in this instance, since the work cannot legally be called a second edition, we delete another number in the code and call it a third, fourth, or whatever, printing."

HEBREW PUBLISHING COMPANY

"We really have no system for indicating first editions."

WILLIAM HEINEMANN LTD. (ENGLAND)

"All our new books carry the line 'First published in 19___.' When we reprint the date of the reprint is shown and in this way one can always tell first editions."

HERALD PRESS

"The first edition of a Herald Press book carries only the standard copyright notice.
"Herald Press reprints always carry an additional line indicating the current printing and the date of the reprint.
"I believe we have followed this pattern consistently over the years."

HERMAN PUBLISHING, INC.

"We're too new to have any single established method of identification. However, a second printing is usually identified as such on the copyright page."

ADAM HILGER LTD. (ENGLAND)

"The first edition of an Adam Hilger book is identified as such by its very omission of all identifying
statements. The second edition is marked 'Second
Edition' and so on for all later editions."

LAWRENCE HILL & CO. PUBLISHERS INC.

"Lawrence Hill & Company books contain on the
copyright page of each title the phrase 'first edition.'
It is followed by the month and year of publication."

HODDER & STOUGHTON CHILDREN'S BOOKS (ENGLAND)

"Brockhampton Press has now changed its name to
Hodder & Stoughton Children's Books. The information
given below was standard for Brockhampton and is now
used by Hodder & Stoughton Children's Books.

"With a Hodder & Stoughton original we state: First
published in 19___. The absence of any second edition
information identifies this as a first edition. For subsequent editions we state: First published in 19___.
Second edition 19___.

"For a title that has previously been published
elsewhere we always state: Date, Name of original
publisher, and original title. Then: This edition first
published by Hodder & Stoughton Children's Books
19___, and subsequently: This edition first published
by Hodder & Stoughton Children's Books 19___, second
impression 19___."

HOLIDAY HOUSE, INC.

"Currently, most of the time, only the first printing has a price on the jacket."

HOLMES AND MEIER PUBLISHERS, INC.

"Most of our books are scholarly monographs which, as yet at least, have not been issued in revised second editions. If we were to do so, however, we would identify only editions after the first.

"The first printing of a first edition is distinguished by: carrying no printing or edition number. Subsequent printings would be identified by number--Second Printing, Third Printing, etc."

HOLT, RINEHART AND WINSTON

"We signify our first editions with a line stating 'First Edition' on the copyright page and a reprint code that shows numbers 10 to 1. If it is the first printing of a first edition, the line 'First Edition' is deleted and so is the number 1, leaving the last in the number code as 2, or second printing. The same is done for subsequent printings.

"There was a time when we left on the words 'First Edition' but also ran a line stating 'Second printing' with the month and year, but found the above to be more efficient."

HOOVER INSTITUTION PRESS

"Our Press does not have a particular method of identifying first editions. Subsequent editions of a

book are identified by the entry on the copyright page
as second edition, third edition, etc."

HORIZON PRESS

"We do not designate first editions."

HOUGHTON MIFFLIN COMPANY

"Please let me define two words first: 'edition' and
'printing'. In times past a book was set in type every
time it was printed and the type was redistributed
after the printing was complete. This meant that each
printing was a new edition and there could be variations
caused by error from the typesetter or alterations made
in the text by the author or publisher. Therefore, a
first edition could often be different from subsequent
editions. Most modern publishers now print from perma-
nent plates which are photographed or cast in plastic
or metal, so the content of the book should be identical
from printing to printing without change. A new edition
of a book in present day terminology, must contain at
least 6 % new material if it is to be registered with the
copyright office and have the words 'revised edition'
or 'second edition' printed on the title page. Of course
there can be limited editions or paperbound editions in
which the only difference is the style of binding and
possibly an author's signature or some other added
item like special illustrations.

"On our fiction, all of our title pages have the year
of publication in Arabic numerals on the first printing
only. This is removed for all subsequent printings.
Occasionally a printer fails to remove this number
in spite of our instructions so that it does appear in
about one title out of two years' publications on the

second printing.

"On the copyright page we place a line on every book which has the digits 10 9 8 7 6 5 4 3 2 1 and the last number is removed for every subsequent printing. There is a code letter after these words which indicates which of our manufacturers (we have several) has produced the book, as we return faulty books to the manufacturer for credit. From time to time we change manufacturers so we need to know where a particular book is made.

"If we are publishing the novels of an author who has published other books earlier with another publisher and we release the earlier work, our title page and copyright page would indicate that this was a reissue but we would start out with first printing for our publication."

HOUSE OF ANANSI PRESS LIMITED
(CANADA)

"I'm sorry to say that we never specifically identify first editions or first printings of books. So it's only when the book goes into a second printing that you can tell for sure.

"We usually include a line on the back of the title page, toward the bottom, which is changed with succeeding printings. The line usually takes the form:
2 3 4 5 6   78 77 76 75 74
If our third printing was in 1976, then the line would read:
3 4 5 6   78 77 76
for example. Unfortunately, once or twice we've forgotten to erase the numbers on the plate for a particular printing, so that we will have two printings showing the same numbers.

"We know that this sort of slip is the bane of bibliographers and collectors, but it occasionally happens

to us, and, I'm sure, to many other publishers too.
With a staff as small as ours, it's all too easy for one
small detail to be forgotten.
"Rarely, we have made the indication:
First printing <u>date</u>
Second printing <u>date</u> etc.
But we try not to do this, as it necessitates a plate
change for each printing, and since plates are good
for about five printings, this is unnecessary expense."

HOWARD UNIVERSITY PRESS

"Our books carry the usual data on the copyright
page indicating the date of publication. If we were to
reprint a title this would be added to the information
already appearing."

HOWELL-NORTH BOOKS

"We have no special designation, except that subsequent editions (usually subsequent printings) are so
stated on reverse of title page--our limited editions
(now all O.P.) are so stated."

HUMANITIES PRESS, INC.

"We do not stipulate any special designation to
indicate that our books are first editions. All subsequent editions carry the notation 'second edition' or
any other numbered edition which may be the case."

HUNTINGTON LIBRARY PUBLICATIONS

"We do not have any specific way of indicating first editions, except on the copyright page. Actually, although a number of our titles have gone through several printings, it is seldom that we bring out a book in a new edition.

"We do not indicate the number of a printing until it is second or more, at which time we give the date of the first printing, and that of, say, the fourth printing."

HURTIG PUBLISHERS (CANADA)

We have no method of designating a first edition. Only those printings and/or editions after the first are designated. These methods of designation do not differ from any previously used.

HUTCHINSON PUBLISHING GROUP LTD. (ENGLAND)

"We indicate the time of first publication on the fourth page of the prelims of a book with the statement: First published month year (i.e. December 1976)."

I

INDEPENDENCE PRESS

"Any books that we think will be in production through more than one printing we identify on the copyright

page with the system used by many publishers. It is
made up of two lines of numbers. One line is numbered
one through six or seven. The second line is a listing
of the next seven or eight years (the last two numbers
of each year). With each new printing we erase from
our offset press the appropriate number so that the first
number in the first row represents the present edition
and the first number in the second row represents the
year of its printing.

"Sometimes this varies a bit. All numbers may be
placed in one row, the edition identification on the
left hand side and the year on the right hand side,
numbering from gutter toward the center of the page.
Then numbers are erased from each end to secure the
proper identification of edition and year of printing."

INDIANA UNIVERSITY PRESS

"Our only definition of editions is essentially a negative one: there is no marking on the copyright or title
page indicating whether it is a first or second edition.
However, if we ever issue second editions of any book,
we announce that fact in the book."

A first printing of a first edition may be distinguished
from later printings of the same edition by the fact that
later printings are indicated on the copyright page as
second printing, etc.

INTERCULTURE ASSOCIATES

"We do nothing to identify first editions."

INTERMEDIA PRESS (CANADA)

"Our current process is to include on the back of the
title page the number of the edition, i.e.
'Printed in a limited edition of 1000 copies
of which 950 are paperbound and 50 are
hardbound and signed by the author.'
"If we do a second edition we print on the back of
the title page i.e.
First edition, 1975
Second edition, 1978.
"I am, of course, interested in your findings. I
suppose it depends upon the book or the conception
of a book that the publisher has. Is it a good policy
to put the words 'First Edition' on the back of the title
page? Only on books you expect to go to a second
edition?"

INTERNATIONAL ARTS AND SCIENCES PRESS, INC.

"In response to your query about identifying first
editions, it is not the practice of this house to do so.
We have recently begun, however, to identify second
printings with that phrase appearing on the copyright
page.
"If the bibliographic history of the work is complicated, a revision for republication, it is usually made
clear either in the author's introduction or on the
copyright page."

INTERNATIONAL UNIVERSITIES PRESS, INC.

"Unless otherwise stated on the copyright page, the

first date of copyright is the date of the first edition.

"A first printing of a first edition may be distinguished from later printings of the same edition by the fact that it either says 'first printing' or nothing at all. Subsequent printings are marked 'second printing', etc."

INTER-VARSITY PRESS (ENGLAND)

"Our usual practice is simply to state 'First Edition October 1976'. On reprints we usually omit the month, giving just the year date, 'Reprinted 1977, 1979.'"

IOWA STATE UNIVERSITY PRESS

"The only identification of first edition that we make for our books is the identification 'First edition, date' that appears on the verso (copyright page) of the title page. I believe this method of identification does not differ from that always previously used by this press."

The first printing of a first edition is indicated by the fact that it does not carry the designation "Second printing, date."

ITHACA HOUSE

First printings of first editions carry only the copyright notice.

J

THE JACARANDA PRESS (AUSTRALIA)

"It is the policy of the Jacaranda Press to list on the imprint page the date of first publication (which also indicates first edition). Each reprinting is also listed and subsequent editions are noted accordingly. This particular method of identification has been used throughout the history of the Jacaranda Press."

JEWISH PUBLICATION SOCIETY OF AMERICA

A first edition will carry the designation "First Edition" on the copyright page. This method of designation does not differ from any previously used.

THE JOHNS HOPKINS UNIVERSITY PRESS

"First editions are only designated by their copyright date. Subsequent editions are noted accordingly."

The first printing of the first edition is designated only by the copyright date. Later printings are designated as follows:

> Originally published, date
> Second Printing, date
> Third Printing, date
> Paperback edition, date

JOHNSON PUBLISHING COMPANY, INC.

"We have no particular method of identifying first editions other than copyright data for first editions."

MICHAEL JOSEPH LTD. (ENGLAND)

"Attached is a form of bibliography which appears in all our first editions. We have no other method of identification. If a title is re-printed, the date of the impression is inserted beneath the date of the first edition."

First printings carry the designation "First published in Great Britain by Michael Joseph Ltd. date."

JUDSON PRESS

"Our first edition is that which bears the original copyright date and no further information about its being a subsequent printing. When we reprint a book, we add the number of the reprinting and the date of the reprinting. If there is any substantial editorial revision, there will be some note made of that as well on the copyright page."

JUNIPER PRESS

"Juniper Books have the number of the printing indicated on the reverse of each title page. As of this date some are in as many as their 6th printing.

"The William N. Judson series of fine printed books by contemporary American poets are all in first edition, except the first, ASH IS THE CANDLE'S WICK, which is in its second printing. We do all printings after the

first by offset from the original letter press books. All
first editions are hand set and by letter press. This
information may be found on the last page of any book
of a later than first edition."

K

KALMBACH PUBLISHING CO.

"Our firm publishes a line of hardcover books devoted to railroading and a line of softcover how-to-do-
it books devoted to hobbies, especially model
railroading. We have retained all of our hardcover
books in print as they were originally published and
have not labeled them 'first edition.' We have never
updated them or otherwise done anything to create a
'second edition.' We have done this out of consideration for buyers of an original edition, who would
later either find the book they own made obsolete
or face a large expenditure for material they already
own to gain the small percentage of new material.
We do, of course, list the various printings in the
book and enter necessary corrections.
"Out of some 23 softcover titles, about 5 or 6 are in
a second edition. On the title pages of these books,
our usual procedure is to list the various printings by
year (sometimes by month if two printings occur within
the same year). If a book is in a second edition, we'll
then preface the printings by placing FIRST EDITION:
before the list or corresponding years and SECOND
EDITION: before the list of corresponding years.
"In summary, then, note that first editions are never
identified as such within the first edition book. Only
second editions are identified within the book, at which

time the original book 'retroactively' becomes a first
edition."

KANCHENJUNGA PRESS

"All Kanchenjunga first editions are identified as
such on the copyright page. The usual form is an
announcement such as, 'This first edition is limited
to X copies,' or simply the statement, 'First Edition.'
Second or later printings are identified as such and do
not carry the 'first edition' designation. Therefore
any Kanchenjunga book marked 'first edition' is from
the first printing of the first edition. (This information
applies to all titles published 1972 through 1976. The
fact that we've done it this way in the past doesn't
prevent our adopting some other method in the future.)"

KAYAK BOOKS

"I use no particular sign to designate either a first
edition or a first printing. I know this makes it hard
on bibliographers but it also encourages them in their
detective talents."

KENNIKAT PRESS CORPORATION

"Kennikat Press does not designate a First Edition.
Subsequent printings may or may not be designated
2nd, 3rd, etc.
"A bonafide second _edition_ will no doubt have some
sort of designation as such on the title page and will
carry a copyright date differing from that of the first
edition."

THE KENT STATE UNIVERSITY PRESS

"The absence of the words 'First Edition', would
indicate a first edition."

KILLALY PRESS (CANADA)

"As my publications are published to further the
writing careers of the authors and not to make a profit,
there is no thought of a second printing, edition, etc.,
and consequently the edition is not designated. There
never has been any change in policy since we began
publishing in 1972.
"All publications contain the following statement:
Publication is limited
to 100 copies of which
the 1st 15 are signed.
This is copy number_____. "

WILLIAM KIMBER & CO. LIMITED
(ENGLAND)

"Set out below is an actual example of our method
of identifying first editions and the same method we
have always used. (The book in question is British
Political Crises).
First published in 1976 by
WILLIAM KIMBER & CO. LIMITED
Godolphin House, 22a Queen Anne's Gate,
London SW1H 9AE

© Sir Dingle Foot, 1976
ISBN 0 7183 0194 3."

ROBERT R. KNAPP, PUBLISHER

"We label edition on the verso and include printing information for each successive printing."

CHARLES KNIGHT & COMPANY (ENGLAND)

"In new books we use the phrase 'First published (date)', and this is how our first editions may be identified. Information about subsequent impressions or editions is listed underneath the original statement, and this information is generally to be found on the reverse of the title page of a book . . . . Charles Knight and Company have been publishing books since 1833, and I am fairly certain that it is not possible to generalize about previous methods. I know from reference to our library shelves that many books are undated. The method I have prescribed dates from 1974. From about 1969 onwards, any editions subsequent to first editions are described as such on our title pages."

ALFRED A. KNOPF INCORPORATED

"Knopf identifies a book's edition on the copyright page. We do not indicate that a particular work is part of a first printing, but for second or subsequent printings, the information is also carried on the copyright page.

"We have been using these methods of identification for a great many years."

KNOW, INC.

"Our first editions are identified as first printings

on the copyright page of each book. Later editions are
also identified. This is the only identification we
have ever used."

JOHN KNOX PRESS

"We do not have a special method for designating a
first edition. The copyright © 1976 John Knox Press
designates both a first edition and a first printing. If
subsequent editions or printings are needed, these are
specifically identified by the addition of 'Second
edition' or 'Second printing' to the copyright notice.
A hardback reissued in paper carries in addition to the
copyright line the notice: 'Paperback edition, 19___.'"

KODANSHA INTERNATIONAL/USA, LTD.

First editions are indicated by the words "First
Edition" and the date of publication. The number
and date of subsequent printings and editions are
indicated.

L

LADYBIRD BOOKS LTD. (ENGLAND)

There is no method whatsoever of identifying a
first edition of a Ladybird book. The year of
publication is printed by the side of their name
on the title page, but then this same date is
repeated in subsequent printings in following
years. It serves more to indicate copyright

first date of copyright is the date of the first edition.

"A first printing of a first edition may be distinguished from later printings of the same edition by the fact that it either says 'first printing' or nothing at all. Subsequent printings are marked 'second printing', etc."

INTER-VARSITY PRESS (ENGLAND)

"Our usual practice is simply to state 'First Edition October 1976'. On reprints we usually omit the month, giving just the year date, 'Reprinted 1977, 1979.'"

IOWA STATE UNIVERSITY PRESS

"The only identification of first edition that we make for our books is the identification 'First edition, date' that appears on the verso (copyright page) of the title page. I believe this method of identification does not differ from that always previously used by this press."

The first printing of a first edition is indicated by the fact that it does not carry the designation "Second printing, date."

ITHACA HOUSE

First printings of first editions carry only the copyright notice.

J

THE JACARANDA PRESS (AUSTRALIA)

"It is the policy of the Jacaranda Press to list on the imprint page the date of first publication (which also indicates first edition). Each reprinting is also listed and subsequent editions are noted accordingly. This particular method of identification has been used throughout the history of the Jacaranda Press."

JEWISH PUBLICATION SOCIETY OF AMERICA

A first edition will carry the designation "First Edition" on the copyright page. This method of designation does not differ from any previously used.

THE JOHNS HOPKINS UNIVERSITY PRESS

"First editions are only designated by their copy-right date. Subsequent editions are noted accord-ingly."

The first printing of the first edition is designated only by the copyright date. Later printings are desig-nated as follows:

> Originally published, date
> Second Printing, date
> Third Printing, date
> Paperback edition, date

JOHNSON PUBLISHING COMPANY, INC.

"We have no particular method of identifying first editions other than copyright data for first editions."

MICHAEL JOSEPH LTD. (ENGLAND)

"Attached is a form of bibliography which appears in all our first editions. We have no other method of identification. If a title is re-printed, the date of the impression is inserted beneath the date of the first edition."
First printings carry the designation "First published in Great Britain by Michael Joseph Ltd. date."

JUDSON PRESS

"Our first edition is that which bears the original copyright date and no further information about its being a subsequent printing. When we reprint a book, we add the number of the reprinting and the date of the reprinting. If there is any substantial editorial revision, there will be some note made of that as well on the copyright page."

JUNIPER PRESS

"Juniper Books have the number of the printing indicated on the reverse of each title page. As of this date some are in as many as their 6th printing.
"The William N. Judson series of fine printed books by contemporary American poets are all in first edition, except the first, ASH IS THE CANDLE'S WICK, which is in its second printing. We do all printings after the

first by offset from the original letter press books. All first editions are hand set and by letter press. This information may be found on the last page of any book of a later than first edition."

K

KALMBACH PUBLISHING CO.

"Our firm publishes a line of hardcover books devoted to railroading and a line of softcover how-to-do-it books devoted to hobbies, especially model railroading. We have retained all of our hardcover books in print as they were originally published and have not labeled them 'first edition.' We have never updated them or otherwise done anything to create a 'second edition.' We have done this out of consideration for buyers of an original edition, who would later either find the book they own made obsolete or face a large expenditure for material they already own to gain the small percentage of new material. We do, of course, list the various printings in the book and enter necessary corrections.

"Out of some 23 softcover titles, about 5 or 6 are in a second edition. On the title pages of these books, our usual procedure is to list the various printings by year (sometimes by month if two printings occur within the same year). If a book is in a second edition, we'll then preface the printings by placing FIRST EDITION: before the list or corresponding years and SECOND EDITION: before the list of corresponding years.

"In summary, then, note that first editions are never identified as such within the first edition book. Only second editions are identified within the book, at which time the original book 'retroactively' becomes a first edition."

KANCHENJUNGA PRESS

"All Kanchenjunga first editions are identified as such on the copyright page. The usual form is an announcement such as, 'This first edition is limited to X copies,' or simply the statement, 'First Edition.' Second or later printings are identified as such and do not carry the 'first edition' designation. Therefore any Kanchenjunga book marked 'first edition' is from the first printing of the first edition. (This information applies to all titles published 1972 through 1976. The fact that we've done it this way in the past doesn't prevent our adopting some other method in the future.)"

KAYAK BOOKS

"I use no particular sign to designate either a first edition or a first printing. I know this makes it hard on bibliographers but it also encourages them in their detective talents."

KENNIKAT PRESS CORPORATION

"Kennikat Press does not designate a First Edition. Subsequent printings may or may not be designated 2nd, 3rd, etc.

"A bonafide second edition will no doubt have some sort of designation as such on the title page and will carry a copyright date differing from that of the first edition."

THE KENT STATE UNIVERSITY PRESS

"The absence of the words 'First Edition', would indicate a first edition."

KILLALY PRESS (CANADA)

"As my publications are published to further the writing careers of the authors and not to make a profit, there is no thought of a second printing, edition, etc., and consequently the edition is not designated. There never has been any change in policy since we began publishing in 1972.
  "All publications contain the following statement:
              Publication is limited
              to 100 copies of which
              the 1st 15 are signed.
 .   This is copy number_____. "

WILLIAM KIMBER & CO. LIMITED (ENGLAND)

"Set out below is an actual example of our method of identifying first editions and the same method we have always used. (The book in question is British Political Crises).
              First published in 1976 by
          WILLIAM KIMBER & CO. LIMITED
        Godolphin House, 22a Queen Anne's Gate,
                London SW1H 9AE

            © Sir Dingle Foot, 1976
            ISBN 0 7183 0194 3."

ROBERT R. KNAPP, PUBLISHER

"We label edition on the verso and include printing information for each successive printing."

CHARLES KNIGHT & COMPANY (ENGLAND)

"In new books we use the phrase 'First published (date)', and this is how our first editions may be identified. Information about subsequent impressions or editions is listed underneath the original statement, and this information is generally to be found on the reverse of the title page of a book . . . . Charles Knight and Company have been publishing books since 1833, and I am fairly certain that it is not possible to generalize about previous methods. I know from reference to our library shelves that many books are undated. The method I have prescribed dates from 1974. From about 1969 onwards, any editions subsequent to first editions are described as such on our title pages."

ALFRED A. KNOPF INCORPORATED

"Knopf identifies a book's edition on the copyright page. We do not indicate that a particular work is part of a first printing, but for second or subsequent printings, the information is also carried on the copyright page.

"We have been using these methods of identification for a great many years."

KNOW, INC.

"Our first editions are identified as first printings

on the copyright page of each book. Later editions are
also identified. This is the only identification we
have ever used."

JOHN KNOX PRESS

"We do not have a special method for designating a
first edition. The copyright © 1976 John Knox Press
designates both a first edition and a first printing. If
subsequent editions or printings are needed, these are
specifically identified by the addition of 'Second
edition' or 'Second printing' to the copyright notice.
A hardback reissued in paper carries in addition to the
copyright line the notice: 'Paperback edition, 19__.'"

KODANSHA INTERNATIONAL/USA, LTD.

First editions are indicated by the words "First
Edition" and the date of publication. The number
and date of subsequent printings and editions are
indicated.

L

LADYBIRD BOOKS LTD. (ENGLAND)

There is no method whatsoever of identifying a
first edition of a Ladybird book. The year of
publication is printed by the side of their name
on the title page, but then this same date is
repeated in subsequent printings in following
years. It serves more to indicate copyright

protection than a method to designate a first edition.

LANSDOWNE PRESS (AUSTRALIA)

"Our imprint page identifies editions in the following
format:
  Lansdowne Editions
  (a division of Paul Hamlyn Pty Ltd)
  37 Little Bourke Street, Melbourne 3000
  © (Author)
  First published 1974
"If there are reprints on subsequent editions we would
run under
  First published 1974
  Reprinted 1975 (twice)
  Reprinted 1976
  Reprinted 1976
"With limited editions we state this on the imprint
page and on a recto page of the prelims, usually after
the title page.
"We will probably move any certificate of limitations
to the final verso page in the future."

SEYMOUR LAWRENCE INCORPORATED

"First editions of Delacorte Press/Seymour Lawrence
titles are identified by the words 'first printing' on the
copyright page. In the case of translations, we use
the designation 'first American edition' or 'first
American printing.'"

LAWRENCE & WISHART LTD. (ENGLAND)

"We have no special way of designating first

editions, except that on any subsequent printing, or
new editions, the previous history is always given on
the verso of the title page. Therefore it is, in fact,
possible to identify if a particular copy is of the first
edition."

LEICESTER UNIVERSITY PRESS (ENGLAND)

"We print 'First published in 1976 by Leicester
University Press' on the reverse of the title page of
the first edition of our books, with the appropriate
date, of course. This is the procedure we have
followed for many years."

LES FEMMES PUBLISHING

See Celestial Arts

LIBRA PUBLISHERS, INC.

"We use no identifying method."

THE LIGHTNING TREE

"It took me some time to decide how to indicate first
editions of TLT books. I have started including a
FIRST PRINTING line on the copyright page to satisfy
that need. Subsequent printings are appropriately
marked by the number of the printing.

"For the books published with no indication, one can
be sure they are first editions. We drop in the second
printing, etc., line if they are reprinted.

"But I must add the caveat that there is no way of

telling which binding of which edition one might have.
As do many small publishers, we frequently print
larger quantities of books than we may bind. Since
we print most of our own books in-house, but have
all binding jobbed out, it is to our economic advantage
to print larger editions, and have them bound depending
on sales. Especially true of case bound books which
we usually have bound in Texas plants."

LINDSEY PRESS (ENGLAND)

"We are a very small publisher, and none of our books
runs to more than one edition, therefore we do not
identify first editions."

J.B. LIPPINCOTT COMPANY

"For trade books, first editions are designated by
'First Edition' printed on copyright page, with or without
the number sequence '9 8 7 6 5 4 3 2 1.' Second
printings of first editions are designated in one of two
ways: Either 'Second Printing' is substituted for 'First
Edition' or 'First Edition' is retained with the number
sequence '9 8 7 6 5 4 3 2' (the 1 being omitted)."

LIVERIGHT PUBLISHING CORPORATION

"Liveright Publishing Corporation is now a wholly
owned subsidiary of W.W. Norton & Company, Inc.
For both Liveright and Norton books we currently indicate first editions with a series of numbers 1 through
9 on the copyright page. A first edition has all of the
numbers. The second printing is indicated by the
deletion of the number 1. The third by the deletion
of number 2, and so on. An actual new edition is

indicated either by the words 'revised edition,' or
'second edition.' . . . From house to house the practice varies and we ourselves in years past have indicated first editions with the words 'first edition.'"

LIVERPOOL UNIVERSITY PRESS
(ENGLAND)

"We do not have any particular method of identification for first editions. We publish books for use
in University teaching and research and normally we
are not concerned with identifying first publication,
other than by mentioning this and listing subsequent
printings or editions in the usual way on the copyright
page, which is the verso of the title page."

LLEWELLYN PUBLICATIONS

"On the copyright page we put 'First Edition, date.'
If it is a second printing of a first edition, we add under
'First Edition' 'Second Printing, date.' We also change
the date on the title page of successive printings of a
book, so that discrepancy between the date on the title
page and that on the copyright page would be a clue
that the book is a subsequent printing of an edition.
In the past, we have not been careful to distinguish
between new printings and new editions, and so the
copyright page might list first, second, third, etc.,
editions, when what is meant is first edition, second
printing, third printing. Whenever we move to a second
edition, that fact is indicated on the title page, so
that if there is no statement on the title page that the
book is a second or third edition, then it can be
assumed that it is a first edition."

LONGMAN, INC.

"Normally we make it a practice to include the legend 'First Published In . . .' on the verso of the title page of all first editions. This is definitely true of all books published under the Longman imprint. It is true for most books published under our Churchill Livingstone imprint (medical), but it is not the case with Oliver & Boyd publications.
"However, with all three imprints all subsequent printings or editions are clearly identified."

LOTHROP, LEE & SHEPARD COMPANY

"We print a strip of code numbers on the copyright page to designate the printing. For a first printing it reads:
1 2 3 4 5 6 7 8 9 10
"For the second printing, the number '1' is knocked off, and so on. Heretofore we have had a different designation including the year, as:
1 2 3 4 5 80 79 78 77 76
"In this case, the two end numbers (the printing and the year) are knocked off each time.
"There is only one printing of each edition; there rarely are any changes, such as corrections , to be made, so except for the code strip each edition is exactly like the previous ones."

LOTUS PRESS

"We are still a very small company and so far have published only first editions, with the exception of Star by Star which originally came out as a hardcover first edition with another company. We have no imme-

diate plans for issuing other than first editions at this
time."

LOUSIANA STATE UNIVERSITY PRESS

"We do not use any method of identifying our books
as first editions. The only thing we do is indicate
subsequent printings or editions by date or the words
'Revised edition,' if such is the case, or 'Second
edition,' if there has been no substantial revision of
the first edition. The assumption regarding our books,
thus, would be that they are first editions, unless
otherwise described."

LOYOLA UNIVERSITY PRESS

"The absence of any identifying statement does indicate a first edition. However, reprinting without revision is not indicated. So a 'first edition' may go
through a number of reprintings. When a book is revised or substantially changed, that fact is noted, and
a new copyright year is printed."

LUTTERWORTH PRESS (ENGLAND)

"Our only method of identifying first editions is by
stating the fact, though the wording does vary depending
on the circumstances. For instance the bibliography
might read:
 First published 19___
 First paperback edition 19___
 First published in Great Britain 19___
 First published in this collected form 19___ etc."

M

MC CLELLAND AND STEWART LIMITED (CANADA)

McClelland and Stewart has no specific designation for a first edition. All reprintings or editions are indicated on the copyright page. While this practice is usually consistent, there are exceptions.

MACMILLAN PUBLISHING CO., INC.

"If I understand your use of the term 'first impressions' as meaning what we would call the 'first printing' of a new title, the answer to your question is simple.

"On the reverse side of the title page where all the copyright information is recorded you will find, in all Macmillan titles (for books published in 1976 for example) the statement 'First Printing 1976.' This has been and will continue to be our method of identification of first printings on new titles."

MC NALLY & LOFTIN, PUBLISHERS

"We've never paid any heed to this aspect of our work. Some of our books are now in their 17th or 18th printing. I'd have to spend a week in trying to figure out my own first editions."

MADRONA PRESS, INC.

"Our first editions carry the notation 'First Edition' on the copyright page. Any subsequent printings carry the notation 'Second Printing 1975' or 'Third Printing 1976' etc. also on the copyright page. We have only done second and third printings, and no further editions on any of our books."

THE MAIN STREET PRESS

"No, we have no particular manner in which to indicate first editions, other than the usual 'FIRST PRINTING' on the copyright page."

MANCHESTER UNIVERSITY PRESS
(ENGLAND)

"As a matter of fact we don't really have anything to identify our first editions: it is only reprints or subsequent editions that are identified by some such statement as 'reprinted 1976', or 'Second edition 1976', or 'Second, revised, edition 1976'."

MARTIN BRIAN & O'KEEFFE LTD.
(ENGLAND)

"Our first editions are identified quite simply, by the words 'First published in (year) by Martin Brian & O'Keeffe Ltd. 37 Museum Street London WC1', followed by 'Copyright (©) (name of author) (year).'"

PETER MARTIN ASSOCIATES LIMITED
(CANADA)

"Our practice here is to designate only editions after the first (second edition, etc.); we do not designate printings."

THE MEDICI SOCIETY LTD. (ENGLAND)

"In answer to your query: no, we do not identify first editions of our children's books and art books. The Publisher's copyright line carries the year of first publication and is repeated unchanged in subsequent imressions. If we made any revisions in a particular title, we would print, for instance, Revised, 1976."

MELBOURNE UNIVERSITY PRESS
(AUSTRALIA)

"Our method of identifying first editions is quite simply to place upon the imprint page (the title page verso) the words 'First published 1976' (or whatever year the publication first appeared)."

MEMPHIS STATE UNIVERSITY PRESS

"We do not indicate 'first editions' as such but do indicate subsequent 'printings' and editions and revisions as they occur."

JULIAN MESSNER

"We do not identify a first edition. Subsequent reprintings bear the notation Second printing, 1977 or whatever, etc."

THE METROPOLITAN MUSEUM OF ART

"This institution rarely produces a second edition,
but often produces second and third printings of a first
edition. In a second printing . . . we ordinarily make
corrections in text or illustrations, whether minor or
major, without calling attention to same. It would be
routine, therefore, to expect some differences between
first and second printings. In a current instance, our
second printing of a book involves issuing copies in
dust jackets, whereas the same book when first published, was put jacketless into a slipcase. In another
instance, illustrations printed originally in one black
(one pass through the press), are printed in two blacks
(a second press pass) in the second printing to improve
the quality of the reproduction. In any of these cases,
the original copyright date (or printing date, if the book
was produced for us abroad) will tell the scholar that
he is holding the first edition in hand. We routinely
print the year and 'second printing,' etc., on the
copyright page or in the colophon notice when we reprint.
This method of identification does not differ from any
previously used.

METROPOLITAN PRESS

See Binford & Mort

HARVEY MILLER PUBLISHERS (ENGLAND)

"We do not identify the first printing in any special

way. The imprint page bears the copyright notice and date.

"Subsequent printings would bear the date of the first publication and the date of the reprint or new edition. So that, unless otherwise stated, the book would be a first edition."

J. GARNET MILLER LTD. (ENGLAND)

"What we put in first editions is 'First published by J. Garnet Miller Ltd. in 19..'

"A subsequent printing would retain this and have '2nd Impression', or '2nd Edition' added. This material appears on the back of the title page.

"We have another firm at this address called The Actinic Press, Ltd., which is a medical publisher, and has done books since 1955 in this way. But it is possible that some titles published earlier had a different wording."

MILLS & BOON LIMITED (ENGLAND)

First impressions are designated by the words "First published 19__" on the copyright page.

MINNESOTA HISTORICAL SOCIETY

"We have no particular method of identifying first editions. Generally, with us if the edition is not specified, it is probably a first, since we do customarily list 'second printing,' 'third printing,' etc."

THE MIT PRESS

"All first editions at the MIT Press include a copyright page (generally page iv of the front matter) to indicate that the material in the book has not been published before. Revised or subsequent editions of a book also have their own copyright date (through the Library of Congress). Any time material is added or changed in a book, it must receive a new copyright. Later editions of a book will often list the publication year of first, second, third printings, etc."

MOCKINGBIRD BOOKS INC.

"At the present time Mockingbird Books publishes only paperback books. We identify the first and each subsequent printing by date on the copyright page, e.g.
First Printing: January, 1976
Second Printing: June, 1976
and so on."

MOJAVE BOOKS

"All information as to the printing history of our books is contained on the copyright pages of our books. The distinguishing characteristics are as follows:
a. All first editions bear only the copyright date.
b. All subsequent printings and impressions of that edition are described in the printing history which follows the copyright date.
c. Editions subsequent to the first are explicitly stated on the title page and are followed by the history of previous editions."

MONAD PRESS
OF THE ANCHOR FOUNDATION, INC.

"First editions of Monad Press books generally say:
'First edition, (year).' In some cases a book will
be labeled 'First U.S. edition, (year)' or Monad Press
edition, (year),' and the year of previous publication
will be given: 'First French edition, 1939' or 'Copyright 1936 by___.' If no printing number is given, the
printing is the first."

MOODY PRESS

"Our hardbacks normally indicate 2nd or 3rd printings.
Thus one without that identification in cloth (hardback)
could be assumed to be a first printing.
"The same appears to be true on trade (quality)
paperbacks.
"However, on mass paperbacks we give the number
of printings only on a select number of fastselling titles
---and this is only a recent policy, so earlier editions
probably do not have the printing indicated."

MOREHOUSE-BARLOW CO., INC.

"Most Morehouse-Barlow volumes are first editions,
since, as is the case with most publishers, it is the
rare title that warrants second and third printings and
revisions. In general, therefore, first editions are
not identified as such. However, subsequent printings
and editions are usually denoted as 'Revised Edition'
or 'Second Printing' or 'nth Printing' on the cover,
title page or copyright page. So it is safe to assume
that in most, though not quite all, cases, books
bearing the Morehouse (pre-1935) Morehouse-

Gorham (1935-1958) or Morehouse-Barlow (1958-present) imprint are first editions unless otherwise noted."

WILLIAM MORROW & COMPANY, INC.

First editions are designated by the lack of any reference to the edition on the copyright page. Revised editions are designated on the copyright page.
Printings are indicated by a line of code numbers on the copyright page. The following line indicates a first printing, 1976:

1 2 3 4 5 80 79 78 77 76

The "1" would be deleted for a second printing.

MOUNTAIN PRESS PUBLISHING CO.

"First editions are not designated as such; it can be assumed that we indicate only those printings or editions after the first."

A.R. MOWBRAY & CO. LTD. (ENGLAND)

"A book is a first edition (first printing) unless otherwise stated."

JOHN MUIR PUBLICATIONS

"We designate a first edition by printing 'First Edition, 19___.' Then we say 'Second Printing' if the book has not been changed. If the book is substantially changed, we say the above plus 'Second Edition & date.'"

MULTIMEDIA PUBLISHING CORPORATION

"1. We put in a new book----First Edition
2. If we print more we put---Second Printing,
   Third Printing, etc.
3. Only if we change content, introduction etc.
   do we note---2nd Revised Edition, etc.--and
   this we put on copyright page."

THE MUSEUM OF NEW MEXICO PRESS

"Our title page imprint has the date of publication.
The c/r page has the year of c/r & only second printings are indicated. '2nd ptg. . . . , etc.' We don't
have a steadfast rule as yet."

N

NATIONAL GEOGRAPHIC SOCIETY

"The Society has no particular symbol or identification mark to indicate first printings. Most of our
larger books contain a notice on the copyright page
indicating whether the work is a first edition or a
later printing. On some of the Society's other publications, the original copyright date, which coincides
with the original publication date, and the dates of
subsequent copyright registration and printings are
marked on the copyright page.
"There is no simple way to ascertain whether early
editions of the National Geographic Magazine are
original editions or reprints. The best information
relating to identification of original editions of the
Magazine appears in Edwin Buxbaum's book 'The

Collector's Guide to the National Geographic Magazine.'

"In the late 1950's the Society reprinted the first 20 years of National Geographic Magazines. The word 'reprint' appears on the covers of these reprints."

NATUREGRAPH PUBLISHERS

"Many of the early Naturegraph titles have been revised, sometimes 2 or 3 times. First editions are not designated as such, rather, revised editions are-- e.g., 'Second revised and enlarged edition.' accompanies copyright dates."

NAVAL INSTITUTE PRESS

"The U.S. Naval Institute does not make a practice of identifying books as first editions. Most books don't go beyond a first edition. Those that do are identified as 'Second Edition,' or whatever. So if there is nothing to indicate otherwise, one can be sure the book in hand is a first edition."

THE NAYLOR COMPANY

"Only one date will appear on the copyright page and if it is a second or later edition it should be so stated."

NELSON, FOSTER & SCOTT, LTD. (CANADA)

"In reply to the above request we practice the

following:

© The Author's name 1976
First edition 1976
Reprinted 1977."

NELSON-HALL PUBLISHERS

Only those printings and/or editions after the first
are indicated.
"Additional printings (or 'impressions') of
the first edition are numbered and so identified on the
copyright page.
"Subsequent editions (after the first) carry additional
copyrights and are clearly identified on the copyright
page. We have no secret codes."
These methods of designation do not differ from any
previously used.

NEW DIRECTIONS PUBLISHING CORPORATION

"There is no way to tell first printings of the early
ND books. . . a few years ago, we began putting
SECOND PRINTING etc. on the copyright page of
reprints."

NEW ENGLISH LIBRARY LIMITED (ENGLAND)

"When we first publish a book, we include on the
copyright line the year of publication, and beneath
'first published by New English Library in 1976' and
this date will coincide with the copyright notice. If,
on the other hand, we buy a book from the American

publisher we will mention on the copyright page when
and where it was first published. In this instance the
year on the copyright line may differ from the English
publishing date."

THE NEW REPUBLIC BOOK CO., INC.

"We have not--so far--designated our first editions
or first printings in any special way.
  "We would note a second or revised edition on the
jacket and on the title page."

NEW YORK CULTURE REVIEW PRESS

"'First Edition'
"Thereafter:
2nd Printing, Date
3rd Printing (Revised), Date
4th Printing, Date
5th Printing, # Copies in Print, Date."

NEW YORK GRAPHIC SOCIETY

"We are now a part of Little, Brown and Company so
we follow their style:
   'First Edition' is printed on the copyright page,
   followed by a code, e.g. 'T 10/76' (Trade,
   October, 1976).
   Alternatively the words 'First Printing' are used.
  "Prior to our affiliation with Little, Brown we
generally used the words 'First printing,' or in the
case of books imported from foreign publishers, 'First
published by___.' If the edition or printing is not
specified it generally means the first edition, as

subsequent printings are identified as 'Second printing,'
etc."

NORTH ATLANTIC BOOKS

"No particular method is used to designate first
editions. Second editions, of which we have not had
any so far, will be marked as such. In the case of
Io, it is more difficult, and a different system is
needed for almost every issue. For instance, in
number 7, only a small difference on the last page
distinguishes first from second edition. Other Io's
like 1,2,3,4,5 state second edition. 6 is also
difficult to tell. 8 is an enlarged edition. But if
you are just asking about North Atlantic, there are
none so far."

NORTHERN ILLINOIS UNIVERSITY PRESS

"In answer to your questions, we have---so far---
no second editions, so we haven't faced the problem
of identifying subsequent editions. All books published by NIU Press, unless otherwise noted on the
copyright page, are first editions. Second printings
(not editions) are usually noted on the copyright
page.
"The preceding paragraph does not constitute a
formal statement of our policy; it is merely a description of our method of identifying editions and
printings."

NORTHLAND PRESS

"We have, since August, 1972, labeled all

our books as first editions on the copyright page of each volume.

"Prior to August 1972 there was no such pattern. Some first editions were identified as such. Others were not.

"However, I know of no Northland Press title which when reprinted did not indicate such on the copyright page."

W.W. NORTON & COMPANY, INC.

"Our method of identifying first impressions is shown by . . . the line of numbers across the bottom of the copyright page. When the second impression is made the number 1 will be dropped from the line; when the third impression is made the number 2 will be dropped, and so on."

NUNAGA PUBLISHING CO., LTD.
(CANADA)

See Antonson Publishing Limited

O

OASIS BOOKS
(ENGLAND)

"Oasis Books first editions are identified by the statement 'First published in (year) by Oasis Books, (address)' to be found on the reverse of the title page, or by the statement beginning 'First published in

(month) (year) by Oasis Books (address) . . .' to be
found beneath our logotype on the page immediately
following the last page of the book."

OCEANA PUBLICATIONS, INC.

"We make no distinction at the outset, either with
regard to editions, or with regard to printings. If a
book goes to a second printing (rare), we will sometimes indicate 'second printing' on the copyright page.
If it goes to a second edition, we will usually indicate
with 'second edition' on either the copyright or title
pages, or both."

OHARA PUBLICATIONS, INCORPORATED

"We do not use any particular identifying statement
to identify first editions. As the books move into
second, third, etc. printings that is designated on the
title page.
"If a book is a reprint that is explained in the
publisher's foreword."

THE OHIO STATE UNIVERSITY PRESS

"The Ohio State University Press does not identify
in any special way the first editions of the books that
it publishes."
All printings of a first edition are indicated except
for the very first. The absence of any statement would
indicate the first printing of a first edition.

OLIVER & BOYD

See Longman, Inc.

101 PRODUCTIONS

"We state the printing date of reprints on our copy-right page. Thus, any book without a printing date, only the copyright date, would be a first edition."

ORBIS BOOKS

"Regarding our method of designating a first edition, we do not, but as you say, indicate only those printings and/or editions after the first printing. This method is the only one we use and have ever used."

OREGON STATE UNIVERSITY PRESS

"We use no special means of identifying first impressions, except that second printings and second editions are so indicated."

ORIEL PRESS LTD.
(ENGLAND)

"Our practice is to state the date of first publication on the verso of the title page along with the date of copyright. Any reprintings, or subsequent editions are noted as such on the verso of the title page."

OUTPOSTS PUBLICATIONS
(ENGLAND)

"All our publications are 'first editions' in your
sense of the term, and all are collections of poetry.
We do not make any identifying statements. We do
give each title a number in the OUTPOSTS MODERN
POETS SERIES."

THE OVERLOOK PRESS

"We write 'first printing' on the copyright page.
We've been doing this since we started five years
ago."

PETER OWEN LTD: PUBLISHERS
(ENGLAND)

"On all our first editions on the reverse of the title
page there is marked 'first published by Peter Owen,
followed by the year of publication.' If we reprint we
state this below."

OXFORD UNIVERSITY PRESS
(ENGLAND)

"Our normal practice, in the Academic Division of
the Oxford University Press, is to give the date on the
title page for the first edition of a book. On subsequent printings the date is transferred to the verso
of the title page, where the dates of the succeeding
impressions are given. If there is a new edition, the
date is normally given on the title page and then for
subsequent impressions transferred to the verso in

the same manner as before. This procedure is, I understand, also normal for the other publishing divisions of the Press."

OXMOOR HOUSE, INC.

"In answer to your query: Oxmoor House does not identify a first edition or a first printing of a first edition of our ordinary books (cookbooks, quilt books, etc.). Our first printings are our first editions. Then we identify second printings as second editions on the copyright page.

"Now in our art books: Jericho, The American Cowboy, A Southern Album Southern Antiques and Folk Art, we not only identify the first edition, we actually number each book of the first edition. Later editions are not numbered and are identified as later editions."

P

PANJANDRUM PRESS

"On copyright page, it says 1st edition. Used to use a colophon in first 5-6 books I published, but dropped it. Also have poets/writers sign 25 copies, numbered, of first edition, for future collectors."

PANTHEON BOOKS, INC.

See Random House, Inc.

THE PATERNOSTER PRESS LTD.
(ENGLAND)

"There is no difficulty about identifying first editions of our publications since a full bibliographical account appears on the verso of every book that we publish.

"In the absence of any indication to the contrary, it may be safely assumed that a book is a first edition."

PATHFINDER PRESS, INC.

"Pathfinder Press uses the following form on the data pages of its books:

First Edition, 1975
"Subsequent printings and editions are listed under the First Edition line, which is retained in all later printings and editions.

"In earlier years we did not list printings or editions and used only the copyright notice and year. We changed our practice after renewal of copyrights eliminated reference to the original year of publication."

KEGAN PAUL, TRENCH, TRUBNER
(ENGLAND)

See Routledge & Kegan Paul Ltd.

PEGASUS PRESS LTD.
(ENGLAND)

"Our usual method of identifying a first edition of
our books is to state on the verso of the title page–
First Published– and giving the year. In other cases
if no date of a second printing or new edition is shown
it can be taken that it is a first edition."

PEGASUS (PUBLISHING)

"First editions are designated on copyright page as
first printing, second printing, etc."

PELICAN PUBLISHING COMPANY

"Pelican has no standard method of identifying first
editions. First edition may have no designation on
copyright page, or it may read first printing. All
subsequent editions or printings are so stated on the
copyright page."

THE PENNSYLVANIA STATE
UNIVERSITY PRESS

"This press identifies first editions only in the sense
that the absence of a legend on the title page such as
'Revised and Enlarged Edition' or 'Third Edition' clearly
implies that a book is in its original edition. The same
is true of printings, since all printings after the first
are so identified on the copyright page."

THE PENNYWORTH PRESS
(CANADA)

"1. 1st printings of 1st editions are not so marked-
subsequent printings are, eg 'second printing'
etc.
2. 1st editions are so marked either on the title
page or in the colophon on the last page."

PENTAGRAM PRESS

"Thus far most Pentagram 'first editions'----all we've
had so far----have been more or less labeled as such
by the wording of the colophon, usually to the effect
of 'this edition is limited to 626 copies, 26 of which
are lettered and signed by the author.' Because I
usually am content to let the first printings sell out,
there has been thus far no need to designate a book
as either 2nd edition or 2nd printing. To my mind, tho,
(& the way I'd do it shd I need to) the 2nd printing of
a book would exactly reproduce the contents of the
first, while a 2nd edition would have the original
contents either expanded, reduced, or otherwise
edited. . . .
"Where I've included neither colophon nor the words
'first edition,' I do assume that people automatically
take the book to be a first edition."

THE PEQUOT PRESS, INC.

"Our normal procedure is to put on the verso of the
title page the words FIRST EDITION. With minimum
or no changes we will list again the words FIRST
EDITION and add the words, 'Second Printing.'"

"When revisions are more than minimal we will list SECOND EDITION."

PERFORMANCE PUBLISHING

"We do not retain a system of identifying first editions on our publications."

PERGAMON PRESS, LTD.
(ENGLAND)

"The only way in which we identify the first edition is the printing of the words 'First Edition 1976' on the verso of the title page along with the remainder of the copyright and bibliographic information.
"This has been our practice since 1965, prior to which the first edition was not identified in any way."

PERSEA BOOKS, INC.

"We print 'First Edition' on the copyright page. We had been using 'First Printing.' As soon as the book goes into a new printing, the designation becomes 'Second printing,' whether or not the book is the first edition of the work."

PHAIDON PRESS LIMITED
(ENGLAND)

"I enclose a copy of our official copyright page which states that a book is first published in such and such a year. For reprints we always state 'second impression 19xx' and for a new edition we put 'first published

19xx' followed by 'second edition 19xy'. This is
standard form for all Phaidon books."

GEORGE PHILIP AND SON LIMITED
(ENGLAND)

"I can reply only about cartographic publications.
"We have no particular method of identifying first
editions other than the biblio and the copyright date
but these we have always taken considerable care to
make and keep accurate. A second printing of a first
edition is rare because we almost invariably make
some corrections at every printing of an atlas and thus
change the edition number. If there were to be a
second printing without correction we would state this
in the biblio thus 'reprinted, date.'"

S.G. PHILLIPS, INC.

"Usually there is no designation of first editions.
Later printings indicate number of printings and date."

PHOENIX PUBLISHING

"We do not identify first editions as such but merely
include the Copyright date, statement of rights and
limited reproduction permitted, LC number, ISBN number,
and names of printer, binder and designer. On subsequent reprintings or revisions we indicate first and
second printings, etc."

PICKERING & INGLIS LTD.
(SCOTLAND)

"Our system is that in a first edition the date appears directly under our imprint on the title page, while on any reprints further editions appear on the reverse side of the title page."

PITMAN PUBLISHING CORPORATION

"Pitman uses a printing line on the copyright page as follows:

1. 9 8 7 6 5 4 3 2 1

"This is the way the line would appear on a first printing of the first edition. For each successive printing, one number would be removed at the right. Normally, after nine printings, we revise or substitute a new line with higher numbers."

PLATT & MUNK

See Questor Educational Products Company

PLAYS, INC., PUBLISHERS

"We don't designate first editions---second and others are stated second printing or second edition, etc."

THE POMEGRANATE PRESS

"We designate a first edition usually in the traditional colophon following the text of the book or broadside.

We generally limit our publications to one printing."

BERN PORTER BOOKS

" *   all publications are marked first edition, second
     edition, etc. as reprinted.
  *   all publications being a first, second, third
     printing of a first edition are marked as such.
  *   as the oldest and largest small press in the
     world we have found it useful to be complete,
     consistent, accurate and non-changing in marks
     throughout the years.
 note: should a later edition be revised over an
        earlier we also mark that.
 note: all markings are on the back of the title page.
 note: all signed numbered editions are dated
        firsts." -- Bern Porter, Chairman of the Board,
        Bern Porter Books.

POTOMAC BOOKS, INC.

Only those editions after the first are indicated.
Printings of the first edition are indicated only after
the first printing.

CLARKSON N. POTTER, INC.

"Every printing after the first is listed with the
edition on the copyright page. (i.e. on the first
edition, first printing, the c/r page says only first
edition; on 2nd printing, '2nd printing' is added to
first edition.)"

PRENTICE-HALL, INC.

"We have no specific method of identifying first editions. We use a printing line of arabic numbers to designate how many printings a book has had:

"10 9 8 7 6 5 4 3 2 1 would be the line in the first printing of a first edition. Subsequent printings would drop a digit from the right. A revised edition would be so indicated either in the title or on the copyright page of a book.

"Before using the numeral printing line we used the words 'First printing,' 'Second printing,' etc."

THE PRESERVATION PRESS

"The Preservation Press has never identified first editions as such; subsequent editions (which are rare for us) are identified as 'second revised editions,' etc., as appropriate."

PRESS PORCEPIC LTD.
(CANADA)

"We designate only those printings and/or editions after the first, and this method of identification does not differ from any previously used."

PRICE MILBURN AND COMPANY LIMITED
(NEW ZEALAND)

"We simply start with
<u>First published 1967</u>

on our first edition, and we continue to add
Reprinted 1968
or
New edition 1968.
and so on, each time the book is printed again (on the back of the title page). . . .

"I enclose a title page with verso from one of our books, and it proves me wrong---we often don't identify a first edition at all. But we add a publication history when it reprints."

PRICE/STERN/SLOAN PUBLISHERS, INC.

"Our form is to put FIRST PRINTING on the copyright page of the book."

PRINCETON UNIVERSITY PRESS

"We do not identify first editions, but only subsequent editions."

PRUETT PUBLISHING CO.

"The only method that Pruett uses in designating first editions is by placing on the copyright page the following words:
First Edition
1 2 3 4 5 6 7 8 9
"Sometimes we do not even use the words 'First Edition,' and the numbers we use indicate the number of times an edition has been printed. For instance, if it is a second printing, the numbers will read '2 3 4 5. . .'"

PUCKERBRUSH PRESS

"I use no designation for a 1st edition. I indicate only those printings/ edition after the 1st. I've used no other methods of identification."

G. P. PUTNAM'S SONS

"Putnam's method of designating first editions is as follows: All editions other than the first one are distinguished by the words 'second (or third or fourth, etc.) impression' which appear on the copyright page. The first edition has no such designation."

THE PYNE PRESS

"We have no special or unusual way of listing first editions. We merely state somewhere on the page listing copyright, SBN number, etc., that it is the first edition."

Q

QUADRANGLE/THE NEW YORK TIMES BOOK CO., INC.

"Our method of identifying editions is as follows:
"We put no identification on the first edition/first printing. Subsequent printings are marked second, third, etc.
"A second edition will usually be identified as 'revised edition' and will not have a printing identi-

fication, as with first editions."

THE QUAIL STREET PUBLISHING COMPANY

"No designation = first printing, first edition
Other printings & editions are designated thusly:
2nd printing = 2nd printing of first edition
2nd edition, 2nd printing = the obvious."

QUESTOR EDUCATIONAL PRODUCTS COMPANY

"Thank you for contacting us re our method of
identifying first editions. Unfortunately, we have
none at this time. We plan to institute one, however,
for our 1977 list and all future books."

QUIXOTE

"We indicate second and third printings of first
editions and second editions, but not first edition
or first printing. Also everything we print we try to
have as an issue of our magazine QUIXOTE, so volume
number and issue number usually show something
about the time/edition. For something we really
like, too, we do a preface or second preface as the
case may be, but we have only had a few second or
third printings and only two I think second editions
so far."

R

RAINTREE PUBLISHERS LIMITED

Printings are designated by a line of numbers on the copyright page.

1 2 3 4 5 6 7 8 9 0 80 79 78 77 76

On the first printing of a first edition, the digits on the left will run from 1 to 9. The numbers on the right will agree with the last two digits of the copyright date, and there will be no reference to a previous edition.

RAND MC NALLY & COMPANY

"As to how Rand McNally trade books are identified, the copyright page carries all pertinent information, including the line 'First printing,' 'First paperback printing,' or whatever appropriate wording is necessary, followed by the month and year of the edition. Previously, Rand McNally used letter identification for various editions, with 'A' being the first."

RANDOM HOUSE, INC.

"All of the first editions of Random House, Pantheon, and A.A. Knopf books carry the words 'FIRST EDITION' in small caps on the copyright page. These first editions are by our definition also first printings. This practice has not been uniformly adhered to during the entire history of all these imprints, but in recent years it has."

REAL PEOPLE PRESS

"So far, none of our books has been altered in subsequent printings. The first printing is indicated on the © page thusly:

            1 2 3 4 5 6 Printing 76 75 74

"The second printing has the '1' deleted:

               2 3 4 5 6 Printing 76 75 74."

RED DUST, INC.

"Every Red Dust Book is a first edition. We have no special way of designating it--If it ran to a second edition--we would say second possibly on copyright page."

THE REGENTS PRESS OF KANSAS

"The first printing does not say 'First printing.' The later printings are so labeled on © page.

"We label a second printing as 'Second printing (date).' It is not considered a new edition, even if a few corrections have been made."

HENRY REGNERY COMPANY

"The Henry Regnery Company does not have a method of designating first editions or first printings of first editions.

"A few Regnery books carried a printing code in 1974: 1 2 3 4 5 6 7 ← PY → 9 8 7 6 5 4. The '1' in the printing row would be deleted in the second printing 2 3 4 5 6 7 ← PY → 9 8 7 6 5 4. The code has been dropped and we do not intend to use it again."

RELEASE PRESS

"We distinguish our first editions with the statement 'first printing' on the verso of the title page. We have not had occasion to go into any printings or editions beyond the first, so anyone obtaining any of our 11 books is assured of a first ed."

FLEMING H. REVELL COMPANY

"We do not indicate on a First Edition that it is the first edition."

THE RIDGE PRESS, INC.

Ridge Press does not designate first editions and never has.

RIGBY LIMITED (AUSTRALIA)

"In answer to your question, we do not have any particular method of identifying first editions apart from a line on the imprint page reading 'First published in Australia 19--'. If the book is reprinted, this line would be followed by others giving the year of reprint. We have not used any method apart from this."

THE RIO GRANDE PRESS, INC.

"Our books are all reprints of rare or scarce books.

"We identify all of our first editions (all of our EDITIONS, really) by a comment just above our logo on the title page--on The Rio Grande Press title page. We indicate whether this is a first printing, a second printing, third, fourth etc.

"Where we have NOT done this, as in the very beginning (1962), there would be an indication of a subsequent printing. For instance, in some of our very first reprints, we indicated the year of the reprint, but after a year or so of business, we began inserting the print designation. So if there is NO indication other than the date, it is one of our first editions. Since the latter part of 1963, all of our editions have referred to the 'printing' by its chronology."

RODALE PRESS

"We here at Rodale Press identify our first editions by indicating on the copyright page what printing that particular edition is. Obviously if the book has 'First Printing', it is the first edition. If it has "Second Printing', 'Third Printing', etc. it is a later printing. Also if a book is a first edition, we sometimes make no note at all on the copyright page as to what printing the book is in."

THE ROUNDWOOD PRESS
(PUBLISHERS), LTD.
(ENGLAND)

"Our practice is as follows: The imprint on the verso of the title page, with the copyright symbol, will show whether the book is a first edition. If the book has been reprinted it will say as much on this page, i.e. 'second impression' or similar. If there is nothing else on this page, then it may be safely assumed that it is the first printing of a first edition.

"Actually, our books are usually the first printing of a first edition, or alternatively an updated edition of a work long out of print, and we always give the most explicit information to this effect."

ROUTLEDGE & KEGAN PAUL LTD.
(ENGLAND)

"Our present practice is to put on the back of the title page the words 'First published 1977 by Routledge & Kegan Paul Ltd.' and any reprint would have, lower down, the words 'Reprinted in 1978'.

"Previously, our methods were more slovenly, particularly in the last century, where the date of an impression was a matter of guesswork and comparing our London and American addresses.

"This information applies equally to George Routledge & Sons Ltd., and Kegan Paul, Trench, Trubner."

GEORGE ROUTLEDGE & SONS LTD.
(ENGLAND)

See Routledge & Kegan Paul Ltd.

ROWLAND WARD LIMITED (ENGLAND)

"As far as Rowland Ward's publications is concerned we publish only our own work on Big Game, and as this is rather a limited field we only handle one printing of each edition which is now published every two years.

"The work you are probably interested in is Rowland Ward's Records of Big Game of which the first edition was published in 1892 and the latest, the XVI Edition published last year."

THE RUNA PRESS (REPUBLIC OF IRELAND)

"We have no method of identifying first editions."

RUNNING PRESS

"Running Press has had no particular method of identifying first editions. We list our printings and their dates on the copyright page."

RUSSELL SAGE FOUNDATION

"Unless the word 'Reprinted' and the date appear on the copyright page, the buyer may assume the Russell Sage Foundation book in question is a first edition."

RUTGERS UNIVERSITY PRESS

"The first edition of a Rutgers University Press book is identifiable as such when the edition is not indicated

on the copyright page. If we have a second or succeeding editions, we indicate 'second', 'third', etc."

S

THE SAINT ANDREW PRESS
(SCOTLAND)

"We use the phrase 'First published 1975 by',
followed by our name and address, the copyright
notice, and the International Standard Book Number.
Supposing that this particular book sells out by 1980
and we decide to reprint it, without an alteration of
any kind, then at the new printing we would simply
add the phrase 'reprinted 1980'.

"In a second or revised edition, the date is omitted
from the opening line which now simply reads
'Published by' and the edition details and dates
are given below the copyright line.

"In all honesty I cannot say that any utterly
consistent method has been followed since the
foundation of The Saint Andrew Press in its present
form in 1954 but the scheme outlined above is
certainly the one currently followed."

ST. MARTIN'S PRESS, INCORPORATED

"We very rarely designate first editions _per_ _se_.
A _revised_ version of a book can be 'second' or 'third'
edition, and _sometimes_ we will add 'fifth printing' etc.
on the copyright page. But not always."

ST. MARY'S COLLEGE PRESS

"We use nothing to designate a first edition in our publication. We do, however, indicate on the copyright page printings other than the first.
"Earlier we did not indicate subsequent printings."

SAMISDAT

"Normally SAMISDAT does not designate first printings of first editions. We do make an exception, however, when we expect one of our books to be subsequently reprinted by someone else. Then the title page of our first printing, first edition, includes the words 'First Edition', usually near our logo & copyright notice. I think we've done this twice, maybe three times, in our 55 publications to date.
"We do designate all printings & editions after the first, again on the title page.
"Most of our first editions do exist in several states, since we often run covers in several different colors of paper, and since we usually use paper plates, which tend to break down during long or difficult runs. (We make new plates for second & third printings, & haven't yet printed anything a 4th time.)"

SAN FRANCISCO BOOK COMPANY, INC.

"Our method of designating first editions is to print the numbers from 10 backwards to 1 on the copyright page, as follows: 10 9 8 7 6 5 4 3 2 1. If all the numbers from 10 to 1 are there, that edition is a first edition. If the number 1 is deleted, it is a second edition; if the number 2 is gone, a third edition; and so on up to 10 editions. Naturally, if the book went

into multiple editions, a further explanation might be
included."

THE SCARECROW PRESS, INC.

"We do not designate first editions in any special
manner, nor do we designate subsequent printings of
first editions. All revised or other editions are noted
as such on the title page."

SCHOCKEN BOOKS, INC.

"We do not specifically indicate that any book is a
first edition. We do indicate on the copyright page of
books for which we have purchased the rights from
other publishers, either domestic or foreign, the year in
which the book was first published by Schocken Books.
We also give the printing number after the first printing."

CHARLES SCRIBNER'S SONS

E - 9.66 [H]

"E is the fifth printing, 9.66 the date of that printing,
H the manufacturer.

1 3 5 7 9 11 13 15 17 19 H/C 20 18 16 14 12 10 8 6 4 2

"After 1972 the keyline was changed to the above
system where the lowest number indicates which
printing, the first letter in the center, the manufacturer,
and the second letter the edition (i.e. cloth or paper)."

THE SCRIMSHAW PRESS (CALIF.)

"To the best of my recollection, we have never indicated an edition as being the first. We have, in fact, generally assumed that the first would be the last. . .

"On the other hand, we have been quite consistent, I think, in indicating second and subsequent printings and even to the point of resetting some of our colophons when the printer or some other major supplier changed between one printing and another. I am reasonably sure that the verso of the title page, at least, will tell the true story: no indication of printing means first edition; any subsequent printings are named as such. Anyone who wishes may verify this with us on specific titles."

MARTIN SECKER & WARBURG LIMITED (ENGLAND)

"Our first editions, and indeed first printings, bear:
First published in England 19.. by
Martin Secker & Warburg Limited
14 Carlisle Street, London W1V 6NN
"Second and further impressions add below:
Reprinted 19..
Reprinted 19..
"Occasionally older books carry the words 'Second impression 19..', but this convention is no longer followed.

"Re-issues are similarly treated (by a re-issue we mean a reprint of a book which has been out of print a sufficiently long time - a year or more; it is not a new edition, there is no new material):
Re-issued 19..

"Second and further editions follow in the same vein
with the addition of
Second edition 19.."

SEELEY, SERVICE & COOPER LTD.
(ENGLAND)

"The Leo Cooper imprint has existed only since 1969
and I think it can be safely said that the bibliographical
details given on the verso title provide all the information necessary.

"Our sister company, Seeley, Service & Co. were in
the past exceedingly lax about including such information in their publications, and I can say no more than if
you have any specific queries regarding books published
under this imprint we would be happy to let you have
whatever information we can find from such files as
remain."

SEPHER-HERMON PRESS, INC.

"We do not put any designation on our first editions
designating them as such.

"Subsequent editions are designated as 'second
edition', 'third edition' etc."

SHAMBHALA PUBLICATIONS, INC.

"Early Shambhala titles were marked first printing or
first edition on the copyright page, later printings
being marked second, third, etc.

"For the past two-three years we have stopped
making marks in our books to distinguish first editions
or printings. However, subsequent editions are

marked so if any substantial changes have been made in
the text or if a book has been changed from cloth to
paper."

SHEED ANDREWS AND MC MEEL, INC.

"Although we have, this year, once issued a book in
a thoroughly revised edition which was identified as
'Second edition, revised,' in the normal course of
things we do not consider minor changes sufficient
to refer to a new printing as a new edition. Thus, I
will refer to first printings and second printings rather
than first editions and second editions.
"We have no special identifying mark for a first
printing. It has become the practice of some publishers
to run the numbers one to ten on their copyright page
and knock off the initial number on subsequent printings.
We have not adopted this policy as yet, although it
might be a good one for us to follow. The only way one
could tell a first printing would be the absence of
information on subsequent printings and even this can
be misleading because until this year Sheed and Ward
had no consistent policy of introducing a line on the
copyright page indicating that the book was in a second
printing, third printing, etc. Our present policy is as
follows: When a book goes into a second printing we
then introduce on to the copyright page the words 'First
printing' and the date and 'Second printing' and the
date. A new line is added for each subsequent printing.
Thus, as I said, a first printing is actually identified
by the lack of such a line. Because our company has
a rather complicated history, having changed
management a few years ago, changed location given
on our title page last year, and changed our name
this year, production records on some of the old Sheed
and Ward books have gone astray and it is not possible

even for us to identify what printing a very old book might be in. In such cases, new printings are being identified as 'A Sheed and Ward Classic' and the logo of Sheed Andrews and McMeel and our Kansas City address is being carried on the title page, to identify the book from previous printings."

SHEED & WARD, INC.

See Sheed Andrews and McMeel, Inc.

SHELDON PRESS (ENGLAND)

"We identify first editions by the following statement:
First Published in Great Britain in 197.. by Sheldon Press, Marylebone Road, London, NW1 4DU.
"Subsequent printings are always identified as such."

SHENGOLD PUBLISHERS, INC.

"With regard to designating a first edition, we do not use any. We do designate subsequent editions (e.g. Second Edition) which appears on the title pages and in some instances, such as our Encyclopedia, also on the copyright page. This is the same method we have always used."

SHEPHEARD-WALWYN (PUBLISHERS)
LIMITED (ENGLAND)

"Our normal wording on a first edition is: - 'First

published 19-- by Shepheard-Walwyn (Publishers)
Limited'. We do not at this stage identify it as the
first printing. However, where the same edition is
re-printed we would state 'Reprinted 19--', and we
would build up the printing 'history' as we went into
other printings of the same edition.

"Although we have published new editions of works
previously published by other houses, we have not
yet published second editions of works we originally
published. It is therefore a little difficult to give you
firm information as to how we would designate second
editions, but I think it is safe to assume that we would
simply say 'First published 19--. Second edition
published 19--.'"

SHOAL CREEK PUBLISHERS, INC.

"We prefer no designation for first editions, but
have on several occasions at authors request put
'First Edition' on the copyright page.
"For all subsequent editions we do put date of first
and subsequent editions."

THE SHOE STRING PRESS, INC.

"Although we try to be exceedingly careful when we
do reprints as to who did the original edition or
the edition used for reprinting, we have not had a
special policy with respect to identifying first editions
of original works.
"We do, however, identify subsequent editions,
although not necessarily impressions if there have
been no changes."

GEORGE SHUMWAY, PUBLISHER

"Usually we provide a statement on the back of the title page such as:
    1500 copies this First Edition October 1976
    2000 copies this Second Edition January 1978."

SIDGWICK & JACKSON LIMITED (ENGLAND)

"In answer to your query about whether we have any particular method of identifying first editions, we can say that if the book does not bear a reprint line, then it is of the first printing."

SIMON AND SCHUSTER

"Simon and Schuster indicates which printing a book is in by a string of numbers on the copyright page, which appears just below the line that reads, 'Manufactured in _____.' If you look at the first number on the <u>left</u>, you will know which printing you have in hand. Thus if the first number you see is 1, you have a first printing; if the first number you see is 3, you have a third printing. This system of indicating the printing is fairly common in the industry. The only difference of opinion seems to be whether to run the numbers from left to right or vice versa.
"The number system was adopted here over three years ago. We do, however, make an occasional exception to this style and go back to our earlier custom of spelling out: First Printing. Some of our books have carried the date of the printing: First Printing, 1964. The custom of spelling out the printing was, as far as I have been able to determine, the only

method of identifying printings prior to mid-1973.

"It should be noted that we use the word 'edition' two ways: (1) to distinguish the style of binding, i.e. a book may be available in both a case-bound edition and a paperback edition; (2) to indicate the version of the text. We do not use 'edition' to mean 'impression' or 'printing.' therefore one may find certain books in which the first number of the string is 1, but the title page and/or the copyright page indicates that the book is a revised (or second, or third, etc.) edition."

SLEEPY HOLLOW RESTORATIONS

"First editions of books published by Sleepy Hollow Restorations may be identified by the appearance of the words 'First Printing' on the copyright page of the book.

"Reprints of the first edition of one of our books will be identified by the words 'Second Printing,' 'Third Printing,' etc., with the date of the printing, on the copyright page of the book.

"Subsequent or revised editions will be identified by the words 'Revised Edition,' 'Second Edition,' etc., on the copyright page of the book."

PEREGRINE SMITH, INC.

"Peregrine Smith, Inc. does not have a particular or unique method of identifying first editions at this time. We do note second (and subsequent) or revised editions on the copyright page of the edition so designated, however; this notation being used when there have been textual changes, additions or alterations in the book. Printing runs have seldom (if ever) been noted on Peregrine Smith, Inc. books."

THE SMITH

"We simply print, on the copyright page, 'First Edition,' followed by the month and the year."

URE SMITH (AUSTRALIA)

"In answer to your question regarding the method of identifying first editions, in the majority of cases since 1960 a first edition can be identified by the words FIRST EDITION or First published in (date) . . ."

SMITHSONIAN INSTITUTION PRESS

"We do not designate first editions. Yes, we indicate only those printings or editions after the first. Thus, it may be safely assumed that any book bearing the Smithsonian Institution Press imprint is a first edition, unless otherwise indicated."

COLIN SMYTHE LIMITED, PUBLISHERS (ENGLAND)

"First editions normally have the statement 'First published in ----'. Reprints always are indicated 'Reprinted ----'. If ours is not the first publication, we normally give as much bibliographical information as possible."

SOUTHERN ILLINOIS UNIVERSITY PRESS

"We do not indicate first printing of a first edition,

but do indicate number-- and give date- of subsequent printing(s). We note revised edition on title page and on copyright page."

SOUTHERN METHODIST UNIVERSITY PRESS

"We do not designate a first edition, but we do designate each subsequent printing and edition. Therefore it may be assumed that if any one of our books has simply the copyright date it is a first edition. A subsequent printing will have below that line on the copyright page 'Second Printing 1975' or whatever the year may be. And this will continue with each subsequent printing. A second edition carries a similar line. For example, John C. Duval, First Texas Man of Letters by J. Frank Dobie has the copyright date 1939 and then below it 'Second Edition, 1965.' We have used these methods of identification from the earliest days of our press."

SOUVENIR PRESS LIMITED (ENGLAND)

"We do not differentiate specifically on our various editions except to have the words, 'this edition first published by Souvenir Press Limited in the year of publication it is'. I hope this gives you sufficient information. We tend to put in the next reprint underneath whenever such a happy event occurs, which actually with our books is quite often."

E. & F.N. SPON LTD. (ENGLAND)

"We do not use any particular method to identify first editions of our books. There is a simple statement on the biblio page of when the book was first published.

If there is no additional information on either reprints or
new editions then the book is a first edition."

STACKPOLE BOOKS

"I'm sorry to say that we don't have any method of
identifying first editions. Generally, our books do not
contain this information, since many of our publications
are quality paperback titles. We may, however, put
printing and edition information in the front matter of
a select few of our titles in the near future."

STAINER & BELL LTD. (ENGLAND)

"We as publishers have no particular method of
identifying first editions. Unless it states otherwise
(i.e. 'second revised edition') then our book is a
first edition - but not necessarily a 'first printing' of
a first edition.
"I'm afraid we have no other more definite method
of identification."

STANFORD UNIVERSITY PRESS

"We do not have any particular method of identifying
first editions. I believe it is correct to say, however,
that a Stanford book is unquestionably a first edition
if its copyright page (1) does not specify 'Second
printing' or the like, and (2) does not carry a line
reading 'Last figure below indicates year of this
printing,' followed by a line of two-digit numbers."

STANWIX HOUSE INCORPORATED

"Stanwix House does not mark First Editions in any way. In the area of our professional books, we do mark each printing after the first. Subsequent editions can be distinguished by their newer copyright."

STATE HISTORICAL SOCIETY OF WISCONSIN (THE SOCIETY PRESS)

The absence of any identifying statement would indicate the first printing of a first edition.
"Subsequent printings of an edition are indicated on the copyright page."

STATE UNIVERSITY OF NEW YORK PRESS

"In response to your inquiry, any book published by this Press may be considered a first edition, first printing, unless otherwise indicated on the verso of the title leaf.
"Our books seldom require recomposition and, hence, nearly all of them are 'first editions.' Second and third printings, first paperback printings, etc. are so indicated as noted above."

STEIN AND DAY PUBLISHERS

"If the copyright page does not say 'second printing,' then the book is a first edition. There are no special marks identifying first or second editions."

PATRICK STEPHENS LIMITED PUBLISHERS (ENGLAND)

"We merely put on the verso of the title page of a new book, 'First published in (date).' This follows the usual copyright notice. Then, if there is a second edition, we add the words 'Second edition - (date).'"

STERLING PUBLISHING COMPANY, INC.

"We merely put the copyright date in without any reference that it is a first edition. Should we print again without revisions, we add 'Second Printing', etc. We have always used this particular wording. If revisions are made, we obtain a new copyright, and add this © date."

STRETHER AND SWANN, PUBLISHERS

"Our first editions are designated as such by the words First Edition on the copyright page. Subsequent printings are designated by number."

LYLE STUART, INC.

"We have no policy about first editions. Sometimes we so identify them and at other times the only way that someone would know that a book is not a first edition is to find first printing and second printing dates and quantities on the copyright page."

SUN PUBLISHING COMPANY

"We do not have any particular method of identifying

first editions."
  All printings of a first edition are indicated.

SUN RIVER PRESS

"Sun River Press does not identify first editions-
we do not identify first printing either."
  The state of a book is never indicated.

SUNSTONE PRESS

"The Sunstone Press uses no distinguishing marks or
symbols to identify first editions. As a general rule
no edition statement is used at all for first editions.
(Alas, there are one or two exceptions when 'First
Edition' has been printed on the verso of the title page).
Second editions carry the publishing history of the
book on the verso of the title page as follows:
              First Edition 1974
              Second Edition 1976
  "Being a small regional press we do not frequently
produce more than one edition of a work. A second
or third printing is so indicated on the verso of the
title page. When reprinting an older title from another
publisher we so indicate. If the printing has added
material, illustrations, etc., we designate it a new
edition and print the publishing history as above."

SUPERIOR PUBLISHING COMPANY

"We usually label our first editions on page 4 of our
books and this would be our first printing also, on
future printings the First Edition is taken off."

SUSSEX UNIVERSITY PRESS (ENGLAND)

"Readers may assume that all our books are first editions unless we specify on the copyright page that the book has been reprinted or is published in a new edition. The date after the copyright sign normally indicates when the book was first published."

THE SWALLOW PRESS, INC.

Both editions and printings are so indicated.

SWEDENBORG FOUNDATION, INC.

"Since our concern is exclusively with Swedenborgian theology and we have a copy of A Bibliography of the Works of Emanuel Swedenborg (743 pages) by the Rev. James Hyde, published in 1906 and containing a complete list and description of all these works in the original Latin and translations published prior to that date, we can easily identify any of these. We occasionally mention the date of original Latin publication, and the ordinal number of the particular reprint of ours, on the respective title page, but not always. Many of these works and extracts are also published by the Swedenborg Society, Ltd., London, which follows a similar practice."

SYDNEY UNIVERSITY PRESS (AUSTRALIA)

"We have no particular method of identifying first edition printings, other than the stated year in which the book is first published and the copyright notice and date on the verso of the title page."

SYRACUSE UNIVERSITY PRESS

" The Syracuse University Press places the following
information on the copyright page of the first edition:
Copyright notice
All rights reserved
First edition
"On subsequent editions, we add the new copyright
date and indicate the number of the edition (second
edition, etc.).
" T h e later printings give the number of the printing.
i.e.:

1st	2nd	3rd
First Edition	First Edition	First Edition
	Second printing, 1976	Third printing, 1977

etc. "

T

TALBOT PRESS LIMITED
(REPUBLIC OF IRELAND)

"In the case of Talbot Press books the incidence of
first edition is usually recognised by the year appearing
at the foot of the foot of the title page following the
imprint. Also on the verso of the title page you will
invariably find reference to 'First published . . . .'"

TALON BOOKS LTD. (CANADA)

"We're primarily a literary publisher and we publish

poetry, plays, fiction and short stories. For most
books of poetry, they only have one printing, which
sometimes is dated by the month that the book was
printing, but, more recently, only by the copyright
date. Second printings usually are noted with an
updated copyright page, on which it says, 'Second
printing,' then the date. Our plays often go into
numerous printings and these are noted on the copyright page, but only as the latest printing, i.e., the
printing history is not given, although the original
copyright date remains the same. Ditto for the fiction.
If we do a second edition or a revised first edition,
this too is noted, but as a continuum, i.e., 'Second
printing (revised),' then the date. The third printing
of a revised edition is noted only as 'Third printing,'
however, the revision having earlier taken place."

TANDEM PRESS, INC.

"We identify our first editions by merely printing
our Library of Congress and our ISBN numbers. Any
edition following the first edition is then named as:
Second edition and the date; third edition, date and
so forth. This has been our policy and no other
method was previously used."

TAPLINGER PUBLISHING CO., INC.

"Our current and continuing practice for designating
all first printings of our original titles is to cite
FIRST EDITION on the copyright page. Subsequent
printings are so stated, as 'Second Printing,' 'Third
Printing,' and so on.
"We also import a number of foreign titles (usually
from England or Australia). These normally constitute

a first American Edition although our copyright page
rarely says so. These titles can usually be distinguished from our own original titles from the notice
'First published in the United States in_____by
Taplinger Publishing Company.' We often do subsequent printings of these books here in the United
States, but not always; however, when we do, the
copyright page will note the particular printing.

"I am sorry that I cannot verify if this has been
standard policy or whether it does differ from previous
methods in the company's early days. But of course
we do indicate revised editions, printings with
corrections and so forth."

J. P. TARCHER, INC.

"To answer your question as to how we identify
first editions: We identify it by the <u>absence</u> of any
designation such as 'first edition.' In subsequent
editions we designate it by 'revised edition' or
'___(title)___ No. 3' (or whatever edition).

"As for printings in each edition, we list the numbers
1 2 3 4 5 6 7 8 9 0 on the copyright page of our books
and delete the number corresponding to the printing
each time we reprint."

TATSCH ASSOCIATES

"We leave first editions unmarked, on the assumption
that if no edition number is specified the reader will
know that it is the first. Likewise, for the first printing
of the first edition.

"These methods of identification do not differ from
any previously used."

TEN SPEED PRESS

"We have no special designation for first editions. We do sometimes indicate 'Tenth Printing' but not always, so that you cannot assume the lack of such identification means a first edition."

TEXAS A & M UNIVERSITY PRESS

"We identify first editions by the statement 'First edition' on the copyright page. Subsequent printings are likewise identified: 'Second printing,' 'Third printing,' and so on. This does not differ from any previous practice here."

THAMES AND HUDSON LTD. (ENGLAND)

"We do not make any special identification of first editions. On the other hand, we do indicate any edition which is a reprint. The result is that any of our books which do not have a reprint line can be taken to be first editions."

THEATRE ARTS BOOKS

"Theatre Arts Books does not designate first editions. We do designate subsequent printings, so one can assume a book not so designated to be a first edition."

THEOSOPHICAL PUBLISHING HOUSE

"We designate our first editions with a statement on

the copyright page similar to the one below.
" 'First Quest Book edition 1975 published by the
Theosophical Publishing House, Wheaton, Illinois,
a department of The Theosophical Society in America.'"

THE THOMAS MORE ASSOCIATION

"No designation is used."

THREE CONTINENTS PRESS

"In all our publications to date, we state very
clearly at the top of our copyright page, 'First Edition'
and we expect to continue to do so in future books.
"A second printing of the 1st ed. will read: First
Edition, 2nd printing (or 3rd-or 4th etc. as appropriate).
"For us, a 2nd ed. signifies a basic change (one or
more pgs. from the original 1st ed.) & 2nd printings
of a second edition would be--2nd Ed-2nd printing."

TIDEWATER PUBLISHERS

See Cornell Maritime Press, Inc.

THE TOUCHSTONE PRESS

"Touchstone does not have a special way of identifying first editions. . . . We do identify different
printings with the simple statement 'second printing'
etc."

TRANSACTION BOOKS

"Since we demarcate second and third editions, and second and third printings on the title page, the simplest way of identifying an original edition is that it will simply have the year of publication and the conventional Library of Congress markings."

TREND HOUSE

"First edition does not have any distinguishing features except that the single copyright line is an indication that it is a first edition. Later we use 'second printing' if no substantial editing or recopyright it in the event there is significant editing."

TROUBADOR PRESS, INC.

"We have had various methods for identifying first editions of our publications. 1) On most of our hard cover books we use the phrase 'first edition' on the © page. 2) On some of our paper back books we used the code '1 2 3 4 5 6 7 8 9 0,' erasing from the plate the last digit remaining on the right at each reprint. 3) Only when it seemed important, we've printed the edition number on reprints; esp. THE FAT CAT COLORING AND LIMERICK BOOK in which we printed 'Fourteenth printing' when that occasion arose. Otherwise we're really not very consistent in noting our editions. The most consistent identification of one edition of our books from another is the change of copy on the ad page (last page) in most of our books. This changes almost every reprinting, but there is no indication of sequence (i.e. you never know, necessarily, from the ad page which edition came before the other)."

TUNDRA BOOKS OF MONTREAL (CANADA)

"We designate the edition only after the first. The only time we show it as a first is when it is a limited numbered edition. If there is only one entry--ex. © 1975, William Kurelek, it can be assumed it is the first edition."

TUNDRA BOOKS OF NORTHERN NEW YORK

"We don't have a special way of designating first editions, except where we say 'This first edition is limited to___copies.' But since we always indicate in later editions the dates of previous editions, where there is no such listing, it can be assumed that the edition is the first."

TURNSTONE PRESS LIMITED (ENGLAND)

"Our policy is to put 'First published 1976' as an indication for first editions of a book which we originate. 'First published in Great Britain 1976' would identify the first edition of a book which originated in America or elsewhere. 'This edition first published 1976' would identify a title which had already appeared in another edition. Subsequent editions or printings in addition to the foregoing have 'Revised edition 1976' '5th printing 1976'."

CHARLES E. TUTTLE CO., INC.

"We normally indicate on the reverse of the title page for any book we publish, that this is the first printing. If we do not make this particular statement on a new printing, we do say 'second printing.'

"In other words, I think you can assume that anything we publish is a first edition, if it actually says so, or if there is no indication on the back that it is a second, third, fourth, etc. printing."

TWAYNE PUBLISHERS, INC.

"Twayne has never designated a 'first edition'. Where a title does have a revised or second edition ('revised' indicates changes of 10% or less; 'second' indicates changes of more than 10% and usually nearly complete rewriting) the new editions are marked 'Revised Edition' on half-title and title pages; a new copyright covering the new material is entered; and a preface indicates the nature of changes. As for 'printings,' it was only in 1976 that Twayne introduced the line 'First Printing' on the copyright page; this line is deleted on subsequent printings. Otherwise, to identify a first printing of a first edition of a Twayne book is almost a book-by-book task that is complicated by the fact that until 1974, the common practice was to print twice as many copies as were first bound (e.g., print 2000, bind 1000), so there are variant bindings. Now we bind all copies."

THE TWO CONTINENTS PUBLISHING GROUP, LTD.

"We do not indicate on the copyright page either 1st, 2nd, 3d, etc. edition or printing."

U

FREDERICK UNGAR PUBLISHING CO., INC.

"The only identification for first editions or first printings in our books is the usual copyright line giving the year of publication. We never use the words 'first edition' or 'first printing.' We do add 'second printing,' 'third printing,' and so on, whenever such printings are done.

"When a book is revised, enlarged, or substantially changed, we will include on the title page and/or the copyright page, either 'second edition,' 'enlarged edition,' etc. If these editions are reprinted, we also add 'second printing,' 'third printing,' etc.

"We have some reprints on our list, especially in the series American Classics, in which we republished or reprinted notable books on American history long unavailable. On such books the copyright information is different, depending on whether the book was in the public domain. These reprints or republications are, of course, not first editions, though they may have a new copyright line if we have added an introduction."

UNICORN PRESS, INC.

"The editions (e.g., signed, numbered, cloth, etc.)

of our hand-printed books are described on the colophon
pages of each book, accompanied often by the names
of the persons who typeset, printed, bound them. For
our larger books, which are usually machine-printed
but hand-bound, the info. you are interested in is on
the © page."

UNITED NATIONS

"All United Nations publications carry sales number
identification on both the back of the title page and in
the tag line at the bottom of either the last page of
text or the back cover. In the event of reprint of a
publication, a statement to this effect is also indicated
on the tag line."

UNITY PRESS

"We have no special designation for indicating first
editions. Subsequent printings would not be so indicated. Should there be a revised edition of a work, it
would be so indicated on the copyright page."

UNIVERSE BOOKS

"First printing contains no identification. Subsequent printings and editions are always stated."

UNIVERSITY BOOKS, INC.

"We show no designation for a first edition, but
additional printings are identified."

THE UNIVERSITY OF ARIZONA PRESS

"At our Press, a book which carries only the copyright date as the date information on the back of the
title page is a first printing. All subsequent printings
will carry an additional line showing the year of the
printing (as well as the copyright date itself, of
course)."

UNIVERSITY OF BRITISH COLUMBIA PRESS
(CANADA)

"In those titles which we have reprinted, we indicate
the dates of the reprints on the copyright page."

UNIVERSITY OF CALIFORNIA PRESS

"We do not use any sort of identifying statement to
designate first editions of our books. We print only
a copyright date.
"We do print a line to indicate such things as second,
third, revised, paperback, etc. editions, although the
wording may vary according to particular circumstances.
"In the past, we did add a new printing line every
time a book was reprinted ('Second printing, 1968' or
'Fourth printing, 1972'), but as that practice has been
largely discontinued the absence of such a line no
longer assures a first edition."

UNIVERSITY OF CHICAGO PRESS

"We have traditionally identified second and subsequent printings of a book, as well as second or later
editions, on the verso of the title page. So if no such

indication appears there, the reader can assume that
the book is the first printing of the first edition.

"Currently, for some books, especially titles we
expect to reprint frequently, we use a double sequence
of numbers, the last of which indicates the year and
number of the impression. That is, for the first impression of a book published in 1976 the sequence is as
follows:

      80 79 78 77 76   9 8 7 6 5 4 3 2 1

Then as new printings are ordered, numbers are removed
from the plate or negative."

UNIVERSITY OF DELAWARE PRESS

See Associated University Presses, Inc.

THE UNIVERSITY OF GEORGIA PRESS

"We do not use any specific identification; however,
on later editions we designate them as second edition,
third edition, and so on.

"Later printings are designated: Second Printing,
1976; Third Printing, 1980, etc.

"If there has been a revision of the book, the
designation will be: second edition, 1976, etc."

THE UNIVERSITY OF ILLINOIS PRESS

"In general, books from this Press which do not indicate otherwise are first editions. Succeeding printings,
impressions, revised editions, etc., are so indicated,
either on the title page (occasionally) or on the
back of the title page along with the copyright notice.
There undoubtedly have been some lapses, but this

has been the policy since 1950. For titles published during the years 1918-50, the earliest publication date is almost certain to indicate the first and only printing or impression in that year."

UNIVERSITY OF IOWA PRESS

"Our press has no unusual method of identifying first editions of the works it publishes. Second printings and second editions are identified as such."

THE UNIVERSITY OF MASSACHUSETTS PRESS

"We do not provide a specific statement to the effect that the volumes we publish are first editions.
"Printings are not identified. We identify only revised editions."

UNIVERSITY OF MINNESOTA PRESS

"First editions of books published by this Press are not identified as such in the books themselves and may be distinguished from subsequent editions by the fact that the latter are identified as such. The same holds true for impressions."

UNIVERSITY OF MISSOURI PRESS

"We rarely do second or third editions of books (that is, with significant changes or revisions from the first). We do, however, reprint books as we run out of stock.

"In either case the best way to determine which printing or edition a particular book is, is to look at the copyright page. If there is no indication to the contrary, you probably have a book from the first printing. The appropriate information should be supplied in any other case."

THE UNIVERSITY OF NEBRASKA PRESS

"The University of Nebraska Press does not identify the first printing of a work as a first edition. However, subsequent printings are identified as such on the copyright page. Thus, the absence of an edition statement indicates a first edition."

THE UNIVERSITY OF NEW MEXICO PRESS

"It is presently our practice to use the words FIRST EDITION on the copyright page of each book. This is the verso of the title page, of course.

"Subsequent printings of the first edition usually carry the word reprinted and a date. A revised or enlarged edition has the words that so state. We do not use any alphabetical or numerical symbols such as A B C D, etc., or 1 2 3 4, etc.

"This press has been in existence since 1930 under a succession of directors, designers, and production managers. Regrettably, the words FIRST EDITION were not always used on earlier books. Seldom was a book reprinted within the same year, so the date of copyright would therefore indicate a first edition if there was no mention of a reprint with a later date.

"Our staff realizes that while the term 'edition' refers to an edition whose text remains unchanged,

and may go through several printings, the average
reader usually thinks of 'first edition, first impression,
first issue, first state' as all the same thing. So we
now state 'First edition' and add 'reprinted 1976'
even if it remains unchanged, or if changed from cloth
to paperback we will state this as well."

THE UNIVERSITY OF
NORTH CAROLINA PRESS

"The Press does not have any method of identifying
first editions. Unless one of our books is clearly
designated as either a second edition or a revised
edition, the reader and bibliographer may assume
that they are dealing with a first edition."

UNIVERSITY OF OKLAHOMA PRESS

"From this year, 1976, on, the form shown in new
books will be:

Copyright 19___ by the University of Oklahoma
Press, Publishing Division of the University.
Manufactured in the U.S.A. First edition."

At the time of the Press's founding, the form used
was the following:

Copyright 1932 by the University of Oklahoma Press
All rights reserved

Manufactured in the United States of America .
Set up and printed in Kennerly by the University
of Oklahoma Press at Norman. First printed
January, 1932

The form used from the early 1940's until recently was the following:

Copyright 1975 by the University of Oklahoma Press, Publishing Division of the University. Composed and printed at Norman, Oklahoma, U.S.A., by the University of Oklahoma Press. First edition."

UNIVERSITY OF PENNSYLVANIA PRESS

"If our book does not say 'Revised Edition,' 'Second Edition,' 'Third Edition,' etc., it is the first edition."

UNIVERSITY OF PITTSBURGH PRESS

"If we are publishing a book for the first time, the following information is inserted on the copyright page:

'Copyright © (date), University of Pittsburgh Press (or author)
All rights reserved
Feffer & Simons, Inc., London
Manufactured in the United States of America

(Library of Congress Cataloging in Publication Data box)

(Any necessary acknowledgements)'

We do not indicate that it is the first edition or first printing.
"If we reprint the first edition, we add: 'Second printing (date)', 'Second printing (date) / Third printing (date)', etc.

"If we reprint a cloth book in paper, we add: 'First printing, (date) / Paperback reissue, (date)'.

"If we have bought the American rights of a British book, the usual wording is: 'First published in Great Britain (date) by (publishers) / Published in the U.S.A. (date) by the University of Pittsburgh Press'.

"I do not believe we have ever published a second edition.

"I do not believe the procedures are different from earlier ones, although minor aspects such as punctuation may vary."

UNIVERSITY OF SOUTH CAROLINA PRESS

"Our first editions are identified on the copyright page with 'First Edition' and the date. All subsequent printings or revised editions are also identified on the copyright page. In short, we normally give all publishing information, including joint publishers abroad, if any."

UNIVERSITY OF TENNESSEE PRESS

"On the copyright page of most of our books we carry the words 'First Edition' in addition to the customary copyright information. As a general rule we do not add 'First Edition' to the information given in scientific or technical studies; however, if the copyright page does not indicate that the volume is a 'Second' or 'Third Printing,' etc., bibliographers and book collectors can be assured that the volume is a first edition. If a title is a 'Second' or 'Third Edition' (a revision) that information is also noted on the copyright page."

UNIVERSITY OF TEXAS PRESS

"We do not state that a book is a first edition. The date in the copyright notice indicates the year of first publication. Subsequent printings are marked 'Second Printing, date,' 'Third Printing, date,' etc. on the copyright page. A revised edition would be so identified on the title page. Paperback editions not published at the same time as the clothbound editions are identified as 'First Paperback Printing, date,' 'Second Paperback Print,' etc. on the copyright page."

UNIVERSITY OF TORONTO PRESS
(CANADA)

"We don't normally indicate that books are first editions. The date of publication is shown in the copyright notice, and if there are further printings or further editions the dates are listed on the copyright page. So that, as you suggest, when no designation is made, it may be assumed that it is a first printing and edition."

UNIVERSITY OF UTAH PRESS

"The University of Utah Press does not have a specific statement for identifying first editions. We do, however, identify a printing as a 2d, 3rd, etc., or as a 2d, 3rd, etc., edition. This information appears on the copyright page, usually beneath the copyright and rights statements, simply as: Second printing, 1976, or Second edition. Of course, subsequent editions beyond the first would have applicable copyright dates."

UNIVERSITY OF WASHINGTON PRESS

"This Press does not identify first editions as such. We do list reprintings and revised editions on the copyright page, so that the complete printing history of the book is given there."

THE UNIVERSITY OF WISCONSIN PRESS

"On the copyright page of each new title we publish, we give the year of publication and identify it as a first printing. Previous to 1970 the year of publication appeared on the title page. On the copyright page of reprints, we give the year of publication and the year dates of the various printings."

THE UNIVERSITY PRESSES OF FLORIDA: University of Florida, Gainesville; Florida State University, Tallahassee; Florida A. & M. University, Tallahassee; University of South Florida, Tampa; Florida Atlantic University, Boca Raton; University of West Florida, Pensacola; Florida Technological University, Orlando; University of North Florida, Jacksonville; Florida International University, Miami

"Printings. There is no designation as such in a first printing. Subsequently we carry on the copyright page 'Second Impression,' 'Third Impression,' etc. Quantities and dates are not indicated.

"Editions. First editions have no special identity. If a work is revised it is designated 'Revised Edition' on the title page and on the copyright page. A second

revision is called 'Third Edition.'
  "The foregoing has been our practice for at least
ten years."

THE UNIVERSITY PRESS OF HAWAII

Editions and printings after the first are so indicated.

THE UNIVERSITY PRESS OF KANSAS

See The Regents Press of Kansas

THE UNIVERSITY PRESS OF KENTUCKY

"Since the vast majority of our books appear in only
one edition, we have had no occasion to develop a
statement identifying first editions. Often when a
book is reprinted we correct errors discovered too late
in the first printing. But we have never to my knowledge identified such a reprint as a new edition, although
I suppose that technically it is that."
  The individual printings of a first edition are not
identified.

UNIVERSITY PRESS OF MISSISSIPPI

"First editions contain our normal copyright and
imprint while later editions carry special notices. such
as 'second printing: (date)."

THE UNIVERSITY PRESS OF NEW ENGLAND

"Our identification of a first edition is in our copyright notice. The first edition contains only the copyright year. Subsequent editions are identified by the
added notice: 'Second edition, copyright----. Third
edition, copyright----.'"

THE UNIVERSITY PRESS OF VIRGINIA

"Our first editions, first printings carry: <u>First
published 19--</u> on the copyright page.
"A second printing would add: <u>Second printing 19--</u>
to the above notice.
"A second edition would add: <u>Second edition 19--</u>
to the above notice, and carry <u>Second edition</u> or some
other qualifying statement on the title page."

UNIVERSITY SOCIETY, INC.

"The copyright date has always been the key to
identifying first editions (our Company was founded
in 1896). Our older anthologies generally indicated
subsequent editions with new copyright dates, plus
a note referring to earlier editions from which material
was taken. There was no clear-cut method of identification, however.
"Today we use code numbers for each printing of a
particular multivolume anthology. For example, 'Pub.
No. 1001' on the copyright page means that the volume
in question is a first edition, '1002' a second printing,
etc. The reason we do this is because in a 17 volume
anthology, for example, the individual volumes are reprinted on a stagger system to accommodate our bindery.
It would not do to have a set of books with one volume

labeled 'third printing' and another volume labeled
'fourth printing;' yet sets with volumes from various
printings do appear. The code is to prevent our
customers from becoming alarmed at any apparent
discrepancy.

"In the case of single volumes, we merely indicate
'First Edition' or 'Second Edition' on the copyright
page."

URBAN INSTITUTE

"The Urban Institute uses a code on the copyright
page which shows the printing, year of printing, and
the quantity printed. Thus, 'A/76/1M would translate
'First printing, 1976, 1000 copies."

V

VAGROM CHAP BOOKS

"Our first editions have all been, so far, 'only'
editions. We would only designate those editions
<u>after</u> the first with proper numbering and information,
to distinguish from first 'only' edition. All our issues
may be taken as first editions."

VANDERBILT UNIVERSITY PRESS

Editions and printings are indicated only after
the first.

VANGUARD PRESS, INC.

"Actually, there is no way to determine whether our
books of the past were first editions or not. Some,
not all, had second edition notices in them. However,
if there was a rush to publication for a second edition
or later this was often omitted. Thus, one could not
tell the difference between the first edition and later
printings. Presently, we do differentiate by numbering
the edition on the copyright page with the numerals:
1 2 3 4 5 6 7 8 9 0. As each new edition is
printed, the preceding number is deleted. Thus a
second edition would bear the number 2, a third
3, etc."

VAN NOSTRAND REINHOLD COMPANY

Since 1970, a numerical code has been used to indicate printings of a first edition. If the number 1 is
present, the book in question is the first printing of
a first edition. The words "first edition" are not used.
Second editions are noted and the line of numbers
are started over again as well.
The same practice is followed for the Professional
and Reference books.

VEDANTA PRESS

"Our early titles simply had the copyright date for the
first edition. Later editions would be so marked, i.e.,
'2nd printing, 1976.'
"Lately, we have been marking our books to designate
the first edition, i.e., 'First Edition, 1976.'"

THE VIKING PRESS, INC.

The usual practice is to have no printing line in the first printing of a book, and to add "second printing," etc., on reprints.

W

WADSWORTH PUBLISHING COMPANY, INC.

"<u>EDITIONS</u>

<u>First Editions</u>. Usually no designation is given in the title. Only designate editions after the first. <u>Subsequent editions</u>. Ordinarily designated in the title as Second Edition, Third Edition, etc. Sometimes designated as Revised Edition, College Edition, etc.

"<u>PRINTINGS</u>

The particular printing of any edition of any book is currently designated by a printing line on the copyright page. The line looks like this:
1 2 3 4 5 6 7 8 9 10----80 79 77 76
The first number on the left indicates the printing (first printing in this case) and the last two digits on the right indicate the year the printing was made (1976 in this example). We did use a different method of indicating printings a number of years ago. We wrote it out (First printing: 1976)."

WAKE-BROOK HOUSE

"Our first editions always state that they are first

editions on the verso of the title page. Reprints are
identified as such. We have not changed our practice
in this since our founding in 1946."

FREDERICK WARNE & CO., INC.

"We identify the first edition of our books by the
following symbolic system on the copyright page:

$$1 \quad 2 \quad 3 \quad 4 \quad 5 \quad 6 \quad 7 \quad 8 \quad 9 \quad 10$$

"Each time we reprint, we eliminate the appropriate
number--i.e. for the second edition, the symbol looks
as follows:

$$2 \quad 3 \quad 4 \quad 5 \quad 6 \quad 7 \quad 8 \quad 9 \quad 10 \text{."}$$

WATSON-GUPTILL PUBLICATIONS

"Please note that we identify the first publication
following the copyright. We follow this practice
whether first published by ourselves or by someone
else prior to our publication.
"Subsequent printings are identified at the bottom
of the front matter by 1st printing, 1972, second
printing, 1972, third printing, 1974, etc."

WAYNE STATE UNIVERSITY PRESS

The first edition is not designated. The first printing
of a first edition is not designated. All editions and
printings after the first are indicated on the copyright
page. These methods are not new.

WEIDENFELD & NICOLSON LIMITED
(ENGLAND)

"We do not have any particular way of identifying first editions, except by the date and no mention of any edition. Subsequent editions state that they are reprints, second editions, or whatever."

WEST COAST POETRY REVIEW PRESS

"We only designate edition and printings after the first--'First Printing, May, 1975/ Second Printing, July, 1976' etc."

WESTERNLORE BOOKS

"Westernlore first editions are undesignated as such. Unless subsequent editions are typographically so noted it is a first edition."

WESTERN PUBLISHING COMPANY, INC.

"First editions at Golden Press, which publishes children's books, cookbooks, craft books and science guides are never designated as first editions. Our printing code is shown on the last page or inside back cover of each book. First printings (first editions) bear the code ABCDE etc. Second prints then eliminate the letter A and so on."

THE WESTMINSTER PRESS

"Prior to 1974 there was no way to distinguish one

printing from another on most Westminster Press publications.

"Starting in 1974 all but the first printings are identified on the copyright page with the printing and the year of the printing, i.e., Second Printing, 1974."

WESTVIEW PRESS, INC.

"We in no way designate a first edition or a first printing of a first edition. Only if it isn't a first edition do we say anything at all."

ALBERT WHITMAN & COMPANY

"Our first edition has no special marking but subsequent printings are indicated by a note (e.g., Second Printing 1976) above or below the copyright notice. Revised editions are identified as such when they occur."

THE WHITNEY LIBRARY OF DESIGN

"I'm afraid we have no special way of designating a first edition. The copyright page simply says 'Copyright (©) 1976 by Watson-Guptill Publications' or whoever the copyright holder may be. This is then followed by a line that says: 'first published in the United States 1974 by Watson-Guptill Publications' or 'by the Whitney Library of Design.'"

WILDERNESS PRESS

"A first edition of ours is indicated by the fact that

it does not say 'Xth revised edition' or 'Xth revised printing' or 'Xth printing.' When it is a revised edition, a revised printing or a subsequent printing, the copyright page says so."

JOHN WILEY & SONS, INC.

"There is no designation of our first edition titles. Only subsequent editions carry a designation. To my knowledge, this has always been our practice.

"As for the printing, since 1969 we have placed the numbers from 10 through 1 on the bottom line of the copyright page. If all of these numbers appear it is the initial printing; if the 1 has been deleted, it is the first printing; the 2, the second printing, etc. Prior to 1969 the system called for specifically spelling out the printing. The absence of a printing designation should indicate that it is the first printing. How diligent we have been in following this routine over the years, I can't be certain. For the past fifteen years, I know for certain that we have emphasized the need to follow this system and I <u>suspect</u> such has been the case all along."

WINCHESTER PRESS

"It is not the practice of Winchester Press to differentiate between or among first and subsequent editions. If there is no indication on the title page, the work is a first printing, however; other printings are identified by number."

WINGBOW PRESS

"Any second printing or second edition is always clearly marked."

WISCONSIN HOUSE, LTD.

"At present, Wisconsin House merely indicates a First Edition with the statement 'First Edition' on the copyright page. Subsequent editions carry the number of each printing."

WM. H. WISE & CO., INC.

"We do not especially designate first editions."

WOODBRIDGE PRESS PUBLISHING COMPANY

"First Edition if no indication otherwise.
"Subsequent editions and/or printings identified by No."

Y

YALE UNIVERSITY PRESS

"We do not identify first editions as such, but any edition except the first has that fact displayed on the title page or the copyright page or both. Second and subsequent printings of a first edition contain a line

stating which printing it is on the copyright page.
This method of identification has not changed over
the years."

YANKEE, INC.

"Usually we simply include the words FIRST EDITION
on the title or colophon page."
Printings of a first edition may not be distinguished.

Z

ZONDERVAN PUBLISHING HOUSE

"As new editions are printed (or new printings are
scheduled) we indicate the number of the printing on
the copyright page.
This does not differ markedly from our previous
practice. On certain books, where the printing
history is rather overwhelming (such as <u>Halley's
Bible Handbook</u>), we do indicate a complete printing
history on a separate page."

ADDENDA SECTION

AMPERSAND PRESS

"The only designation is the date of publication. Subsequent editions or printings would be indicated as such."

ARCHITECTURAL PRESS, LTD. (ENGLAND)

"The form of words is: First published (year) by the Architectural Press, Ltd."

ARLINGTON HOUSE PUBLISHERS

"Arlington House does not designate first editions. However, reprints are indicated in the usual manner: Second printing, May 1973, for example."

CAMBRIDGE UNIVERSITY PRESS (ENGLAND)

First printings are designated by the statement "First published 19__." on the verso of the title page. Subsequent printings and editions are indicated.

CAROLINGIAN PRESS

"All editions are (to date) first and limited to one."

CEOLFRITH PRESS (ENGLAND)

"So far, Ceolfrith Press has only published first editions and this is indicated by simply printing inside the title leaf 'First Edition', followed by the date.

"However, we also published limited editions of most of our publications (excluding exhibition catalogues) which are numbered and signed by the authors, poets or artists. The reverse of the title leaf of these editions is also designated as follows: 'This is No.___ of the signed edition' and the numbering is done by hand.

"We also state in our publications how many copies were printed in both ordinary and signed editions."

CLOCK HOUSE PUBLICATIONS (CANADA)

Editions and printings and their dates are designated on the copyright page.

CURBSTONE PRESS

"We designate a first edition by the words 'First Edition' on the copyright page. We make no distinction between 'First Edition' and 'First Printing.' If we print more copies of the same book, it is labelled 'Second Edition.'"

DIANA PRESS, INC.

"We do not usually designate first editions----only second editions."

DODD, MEAD & COMPANY, INC.

As of December 9, 1976, Dodd, Mead & Company, Inc. Inc. has changed its practice regarding the designation of first printings. The new practice is as follows:

"A line of numbers -- 1 through 10 -- appears on the copyright page of the first printing of a book. On the second printing, the number 1 is simply blanked out, leaving the first number of the sequence a 2, and so on for each subsequent printing.

"Dodd, Mead will begin this method of printing indication with all new books, the copyright pages for which have yet to be set into type. This includes adult and juvenile titles."

DUSTBOOKS

"We simply print 'First Printing' on reverse of title page."

GRAY'S PUBLISHING LTD. (CANADA)

"It could be assumed that we designate only those printings and/or editions after the first. These methods of identification do not differ from any previously used."

HARCOURT BRACE JOVANOVICH, INC.

"I believe our method of designating first editions is fairly standard throughout the industry. On the first printing, the words 'First edition' appear on the copyright page. On each subsequent printing, the phrase 'First edition' is dropped and the printing is identified by a letter: the second printing is identified

by the letter B, the third printing is C (but the letter
B is also retained, so that on the copyright page this
designation appears 'BC'). This goes up to the letter
J. At the 11th printing, we begin using a number
identification: 11th printing, 12th printing, etc.
However, in the case of <u>juvenile</u> or paperback titles,
we do <u>not</u> start using numbers at the 11th printing ,
but instead continue with letters right through Z. If
there are more than 26 printings, we start using double
letters: AA, BB, and so on.
   "If the material in the book is substantially changed,
we will identify it as the second edition, apply for a
new copyright, and begin the same numbering sequence
as for a first edition."

HIGHWAY BOOK SHOP (CANADA)

   "We have very short press runs & no exciting system
for designating first editions. Most of our books are
of regional and local interest."

JEWISH CHRONICLE PUBLICATIONS
(ENGLAND)

   "We have no particular method of identifying first
editions of our books."

LERNER PUBLICATIONS COMPANY

   "In our publications, 'first edition' and 'first
printing' are usually synonymous. A first printing is
identified by either the words,'First Printing, 1977'
on the copyright page or by the following code:
   1 2 3 4 5 6 7 8 9 10 85 84 83 82 81 80 79 78 77

"When the book is reprinted, the appropriate printing number and year of reprint are removed. (That is, a second printing done in 1978 will have the '1' and the '77' omitted.)"

THE C.V. MOSBY COMPANY

"No designation is used for the first edition. All editions after the first are indicated by stating '2nd edition', '3rd edition', etc., after the title."

PARENTS' MAGAZINE PRESS

"Up to the present time, we have not had any method of designating first editions of the books we publish through our book publishing division, Parents' Magazine Press. However, beginning with our fall list (1977), we will be designating first and subsequent editions of our books with a line at the end of the copyright information (and preceeding the Library of Congress Cataloging in Publication data) as follows:
10 9 8 7 6 5 4 3 2 1
and with each additional printing, one number at the right drops off to indicate edition."

PULSE-FINGER PRESS

"We usually identify first editions and/or printings on the copyright page. Where no designation is used at the outset, subsequent editions/printings are identified.
"The methods of identification do not differ from those previously used."

RAMPARTS PRESS, INC.

"Ramparts Press now prints 'First Edition' on the
copyright page of the first printing of each of our
books."

UNIVERSITY OF NOTRE DAME PRESS

"We have no method of designating a first edition."